Schofield & Sims

Maths

Key Stage 2

Guide

Steve Mills and
Hilary Koll

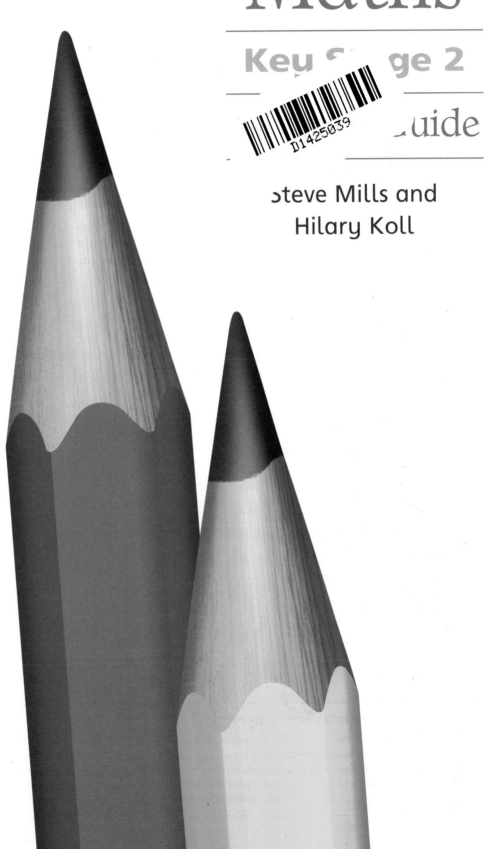

Introduction

The purpose of this book

This book will help you to revise for the maths tests at the end of Year 6 and to get better marks in them.

What you will need

Paper, a pencil or pen and a calculator.

How to use this book

- It is best to start at the beginning and work through each topic in turn. If you prefer, you could use the Contents list or the Index to choose a topic.
- Turn to the topic and read the explanation.
- Study each example. Would you be able to work through an example like this on your own? Think about how you would do it.
- Some of the words in each topic appear in orange. Their definitions are given in the Glossary on pages 94 and 95. Try to remember them.
- The **Remember** section at the end of the topic lists the most important things you need to know. Read it through, then cover it up. Can you remember what it says?
- Try the **Test yourself!** questions. Write your answers on a piece of paper. Then check them against the correct answers on pages 88 to 91.
- Maybe you got some questions wrong, or perhaps you're not sure that you understand the topic? Read it again and have another go at the questions.
- If you get a good mark and are sure that you understand, tick the circle in the corner of the page, and move on.
- When you have worked through the whole book, check whether there is a tick on each page. Are any pages not ticked? If so, you need to go back to those topics and work through them again.
- Read the 'Tips for tests' at the back of this book. Then you are ready to take the tests. Good luck!

How to get even better marks!

- Work through the Schofield & Sims Maths Practice Papers for Key Stage 2, available separately.

Note for teachers and parents

The Schofield & Sims Revision Guides have been written by teachers, for use at school and at home. The Guides enable children to revise independently for the National Curriculum Key Stage tests (SATs). The focus is on clear explanations of the topics covered by the tests, all of which will already have been taught in school. Each maths topic is matched to the National Numeracy Strategy, and all the curricular links are listed in the Curriculum chart on pages 92 to 93. Practice Papers designed to accompany this book will further improve children's test results (see back cover for full details).

Contents

The value of digits

There are 10 **digits**:

0, 1, 2, 3, 4, 5, 6, 7, 8, 9

We put these digits together to make numbers.

For example, **274** is a three-digit number and **3092767** is a **seven-digit number**.

The **position** of a digit in a number gives its **value** – it tells us what it is worth.

The values of digits

Look at this number ⟶ 4 5 1 5 2
The digit 5 appears twice, but
its **value** each time is very **different**.   5000   50

If you're not sure how large a number is – write the headings over the digits.

Look at the number 45152

Here are the values of all the digits:

	Ten Thousands	Thousands	Hundreds	Tens	Units
We can write the number in full like this ⟶	4	5	1	5	2
	40000 +	5000 +	100 +	50 +	2

Now look at the number 7328436

Here are the values of all the digits:

	Millions	Hundred Thousands	Ten Thousands	Thousands	Hundreds	Tens	Units
We can write the number in full like this ⟶	7	3	2	8	4	3	6
	7000000 +	300000 +	20000 +	8000 +	400 +	30 +	6

Test yourself!

1 Write these numbers in full:
a) **312** = 300 + 10 + 2
b) **4839**
c) **69215**
d) **2106387**

2 Write the value of the red digit in each number:
a) **702**
b) **3028**
c) **41256**
d) **702351**
e) **529573**
f) **275003**
g) **2800645**

Think what the number **505** would be without a zero – it would be just **55**. And what about **30500**? Zeros are important because they keep other digits in their proper places.

Remember

These are the digit headings:

Millions   Hundred Thousands   Ten Thousands   Thousands   Hundreds   Tens   Units

The value of digits

We can use the **digit headings** to help us write numbers in **words** ...

Write 3784 in words

	Thousands	Hundreds	Tens	Units
3784	3	7	8	4

3784 ⟶ Answer: three thousand seven hundred and eighty-four

Write 52009 in words

	Ten Thousands	Thousands	Hundreds	Tens	Units
52009	5	2	0	0	9

52009 ⟶ Answer: fifty-two thousand and nine

Write 721936 in words

	Hundred Thousands	Ten Thousands	Thousands	Hundreds	Tens	Units
721936	7	2	1	9	3	6

721936 ⟶ Answer: seven hundred and twenty-one thousand, nine hundred and thirty-six

Large numbers

Very large numbers can be grouped in threes from the right, like this:

31 670 432

thirty-one million, six hundred and seventy thousand, four hundred and thirty-two

Because numbers like this are so large, we often leave **spaces** to make them easier to read.

54 893 091

Adding and subtracting numbers

Make sure you know the **values** of the numbers you are adding and subtracting, so that you add tens to tens, hundreds to hundreds and so on. What is wrong with this sum?

```
  2579193
+  53704      ✗
_____
```

Test yourself!

1 Write these numbers in words:
   a) 351   e) 50 091
   b) 4857   f) 659 234
   c) 2041   g) 2 437 896
   d) 8002   h) 20 202 020

2 Write these numbers using digits:
   a) five thousand, two hundred and fifty-four
   b) sixty-one thousand, five hundred and ninety-one
   c) twenty-six million, five hundred and four thousand, three hundred and eight
   d) one million, one hundred thousand, one hundred and one

Remember

When **adding** and **subtracting** numbers, make sure you **line up the digits** correctly.

Rounding

Why?

We **round** numbers for several reasons:

- **to give a quick idea of a number**

Which do you think is the better of these two headlines?

Man wins a million pounds!

Man wins nine hundred and sixty-two thousand, five hundred and twelve pounds fifty-seven pence!

- **to give a rough answer before we** calculate:
  e.g. 43 × 18 is about the same as 40 × 20 = 800.

To round numbers, you must decide what you are rounding **to**.

The number **66 259** could be rounded to ...
          66 260 (to the nearest 10)
or to 66 300 (to the nearest 100)
or to 66 000 (to the nearest 1000)
or to 70 000 (to the nearest 10000).

> The words **rounding** or **approximating** in maths are usually followed by the words ... **to the nearest** ...

How to round a number

Round 66 259 to the nearest 100

One way is to look at the number and see which multiple of 100 the number is nearest to:

66 200   66 259   66 300

It is nearest to 66 300

A **second way** is to:

1 See what you are rounding to: here, it is to the nearest 100.

2 Point to this digit in the number ...

TTh	Th	H	T	U
6	6	2	5	9

3 Look at the digit to the right of it ...

6	6	2	<u>5</u>	9

If it's smaller than 5, the digit stays the same.

If it's 5 or larger, the digit goes up one.

Zeros then cover the digits to the right.

6	6	3	0	0

Answer: 66 300

Test yourself!

1 Round these numbers to the nearest 10:
   a) 2419
   b) 3504
   c) 5427
   d) 3051
   e) 6499

2 Round these numbers to the nearest 100:
   a) 2891
   b) 8629
   c) 9045
   d) 9054
   e) 62981

3 Round these numbers to the nearest 1000
   a) 62 194
   b) 34 528
   c) 45 091
   d) 74 999
   e) 39 522

Remember

Make sure you know what you are rounding **to**, such as the nearest 100 or 1000. Use rounding when you calculate, to check your answers.

Rounding

Round 6 723 769 to the nearest 100

M	HTh	TTh	Th	H	T	U
6	7	2	3	7	6	9

Point to 100 digit. Look to the right. 6 is 5 or more. So the digit 7 needs to go up one. Zeros cover the digits to the right.

Answer: 6 723 800

Round 2 497 286 to the nearest 1000

M	HTh	TTh	Th	H	T	U
2	4	9	7	2	8	6

Point to 1000 digit. Look to the right. 2 is less than 5. So the digit 7 stays the same. Zeros cover the digits to the right.

Answer: 2 497 000

If your digit is a 9 and it needs to go up one, change it to zero and add one to the digit on its left instead!

Round 6 709 728 to the nearest 1000

6 709 728   becomes   6 710 000

Answer: 6 710 000

Rounding decimals

You can round decimals in exactly the same way as whole numbers. This time, though, numbers are rounded to the nearest whole number, tenth, hundredth, or thousandth etc.

Round 64.78 to the nearest tenth

T	U	.	t	h
6	4	.	7	8

Point to the tenths digit, to the right of the decimal point, then look at the digit to its right

As 8 is 5 or larger, you round the 7 up one, so the answer is ...

6   4 . 8   0

You don't need to write the zeros at the end of a decimal, so the answer is

6   4 . 8

Answer: 64.8

Test yourself!

1 Round these numbers to the nearest 10, then to the nearest 100, then to the nearest 1000:
   a) 5692
   b) 72 501
   c) 30 903
   d) 430 092
   e) 2 652 991

2 Round these decimal numbers to the nearest tenth:
   a) 26.78
   b) 18.62
   c) 56.349
   d) 60.752
   e) 90.061

Remember

Round decimals the same way as for whole numbers.

When rounding 'to the nearest tenth', find the tenths digit and look at the digit to its right:
- if it is **5 or above**, the tenths digit goes **up one**
- if it is **4 or below**, the tenths digit **stays the same**.

Ordering numbers

Which of these football attendances is largest, next largest and so on?

CHELSEA	v	MIDDLESBROUGH	36 239
ASTON VILLA	v	SPURS	42 231
ARSENAL	v	LIVERPOOL	39 327
MAN CITY	v	EVERTON	53 620
BLACKBURN	v	SOUTHAMPTON	36 007

Think about the digit headings and, when the numbers have the same number of digits, ask:

Which number has most ten thousands? **53 620**

Which has the next greatest number of ten thousands? **42 231**

Which numbers have the next greatest number of ten thousands?
36 239   39 327   36 007

Which of these has most thousands? **39 327**

Which numbers have the next greatest number of thousands?
36 239   36 007

Which has the greatest number of hundreds? **36 239**

Which is the smallest number? **36 007**

Answer:
Man City   v Everton   53 620
Aston Villa v Spurs   42 231
Arsenal   v Liverpool   39 327
Chelsea   v Middlesbrough 36 239
Blackburn   v Southampton   36 007

Remember

To find the number **halfway** between two others:

- find the **difference, halve it** and **add it** to the **smaller** number
- **or add the two numbers** and **halve the answer.**

Giving a number between two others

Give a number between 23 854 and 23 671

Compare the two numbers. Here both have '23 thousand', so your answer will also.

- Now compare the other digits ... 854 and 671.
- You have to write a number that is **larger than** 23 671 but **smaller than** 23 854.

Answer: e.g. 23 672, 23 700 or 23 800

Finding a number halfway between two others

What number is halfway between 2346 and 2142?

- Find the **difference** between the numbers: 2346 − 2142 = 204.
- **Halve the answer.** Half of 204 is 102.
- **Add** 102 to the **smaller** number, 2142.

Answer: 2244

Another way (quicker!) is to add the two numbers and halve the answer.

Test yourself!

1 Order these numbers, largest first:
   6291
   92 716
   80 062
   8502
   67 293

2 Order these numbers, smallest first:
   54 351
   48 602
   51 762
   48 701
   50 001

3 Order these numbers, smallest first:
   62 071
   62 835
   62 561
   62 809
   62 831

4 Write a number that is halfway between 3482 and 3164

Negative numbers

A **negative number** is a number that is less than zero. Negative numbers **have a minus sign in front of them**, like −8 and −1, to show **how many less than 0 they are**.

Temperature scale

One use of negative numbers is to show **temperature**.

Look at this thermometer.

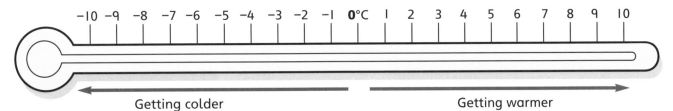

Getting colder   Getting warmer

When the temperature falls below zero degrees Celsius (0°C), we use negative numbers to show how far below zero it has fallen. Use the thermometer to see why −3° is colder than 0° and −5° is colder than −2°. Can you see that −1° is colder than 6°? Find each pair of numbers on the thermometer. On this thermometer, the temperature further to the left is **always** colder.

The number line

Like a thermometer, the number line also shows negative numbers. Use the number line to see why −3 is smaller than 0 and −5 is smaller than −2. Find −3 and 0 on the line. The number further to the left is **always** smaller. Find −9 and −5 on the line. −9 is smaller than −5.

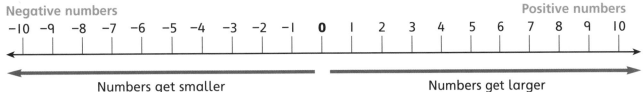

Negative numbers   Positive numbers

Numbers get smaller   Numbers get larger

This is only part of the number line — it goes on forever in both directions.

Test yourself!

1 Which of these pairs is the smaller number?
a) 8, 3
b) 4, −2
c) −9, 2
d) −5, −2
e) −14, −9

Remember

Negative numbers are less than zero, **positive numbers** are greater than zero.

−6 is **smaller** than −5 even though, with positive numbers, 6 is **larger** than 5.

Positive numbers are the numbers we use everyday, like 12, 27 and 100. We could put a + sign in front of them, like +12 and +27, but we usually don't.

Negative numbers

Ordering numbers

We can use a number line to order numbers, as shown below.

> Put −2, 8, 3, 0, −10, −6 in order of size, starting with the smallest

Place each number on the line, like this:

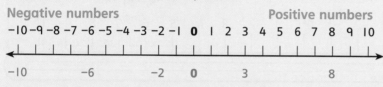

Answer: −10, −6, −2, 0, 3, 8

> Put 7, −1, −3, 10, −8, −5 in order of size, starting with the largest

Place each number on the line, like this:

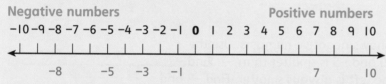

Answer: 10, 7, −1, −3, −5, −8

Finding the difference between numbers

> At 10 a.m. the temperature in the freezer was −10°C. At 4 p.m. it was −2°C. What was the difference in temperatures?

- Find the numbers on the line.
- Count from one to the other – count the jumps, not the marks!

Negative numbers   Positive numbers

−10 −9 −8 −7 −6 −5 −4 −3 −2 −1   0   1   2   3   4   5   6   7   8   9   10

8 places to the left

Answer: The difference was 8°C.

Test yourself!

1   Put these numbers in order of size, starting with the smallest:

a) 6, −2, 4, 0, 7

b) 2, −9, 4, 3, −1

c) −4, 4, −7, −2, 10

d) −5, −2, −15, 7, −1

e) −1, −12, −54, −23, −6

2   a)

> At 6 a.m. the temperature was −9°C. At 2 p.m. it was −1°C.

What was the difference in temperatures?

b)

> At noon the temperature was 8°C. At 6 p.m. it was −5°C.

What was the difference in temperatures?

Remember

When ordering or finding the difference between temperatures, draw a number line.

Negative numbers

Find the difference between 2 and –3

Negative numbers   Positive numbers

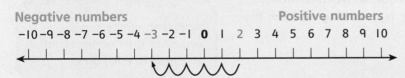

Answer: **There is a difference of 5 places, so the difference is 5.**

Subtracting positive and negative numbers

Start at the first number and count along the number line **to the left**.

The temperature was –4°C and it fell by 5°C.
What is the new temperature?

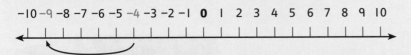

Answer: **The new temperature is –9° because –4 subtract 5 = –9.**

Use this method to find temperature **falls**. If the fall crosses zero, use zero as a 'stepping stone', as in the example below.

The temperature was 8°C and it fell by 12°C.
What is the new temperature?

–10 –9 –8 –7 –6 –5 –4 –3 –2 –1 **0** 1 2 3 4 5 6 7 8 9 10

4 places + 8 places = 12 places

Answer: **The new temperature is –4°.**

Adding positive and negative numbers

Start at the first number and count along the number line **to the right**.

The temperature was –6°C and it rose by 10°C.
What is the new temperature?

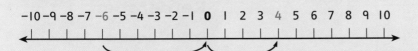

Answer: **10 places = 6 places + 4 places, so the new temperature is 4°C.**

Use the method above to find temperature **rises**.

Test yourself!

1 Find the difference between:
  a) 3 and –4
  b) 5 and –7
  c) –3 and 6
  d) –4 and –9
  e) –1 and –10

2 Use a number line to solve these:
  a) –4 – 3
  b) –2 – 6
  c) –1 – 7
  d) –8 – 3
  e) –6 – 6

3 Use a number line to solve these:
  a) –5 + 4
  b) –3 + 2
  c) –4 + 8
  d) –2 + 9
  e) –5 + 7

Remember

Think of temperature rises as + and temperature falls as –.

Use a number line like this:

- when **subtracting,** move to the **left**
- when **adding,** move to the **right.**

Number sequences

Continuing number sequences

To continue these patterns, find the **difference between** adjacent numbers in the sequence by **subtracting** or by **counting on** from the smaller number.

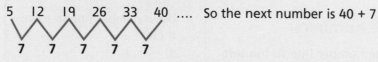

Continue the sequence 5 12 19 26 33 40 ...

In this sequence, the **difference number** is the same:

5   12   19   26   33   40 ....   So the next number is 40 + 7
  7   7   7   7   7

Answer: **47**

Continue the sequence 37 29 22 16 11 7 ...

In this second sequence, there is a **pattern**:

37 29   22   16   11   7 ....   So the next number is 7 – 3
    8   7   6   5   4

Answer: **4**

Explaining number sequences

When asked to explain a number **sequence** or pattern:

- use **numbers** in your explanation
- use **words** like 'difference', 'larger', 'smaller', 'decreasing', descending, 'increasing', ascending ...

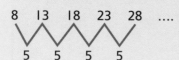

Explain this pattern: 8 13 18 23 28

8   13   18   23   28 ....
  5   5   5   5

Answer: The first number is 8. The numbers in this sequence get **larger by a difference of 5** each time.

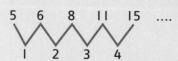

Now explain this second pattern: 5 6 8 11 15

5   6   8   11   15 ....
  1   2   3   4

Answer: The first number is 5. The difference between each number in this sequence **increases by 1** each time. The difference goes 1, 2, 3, 4, and so on.

Test yourself!

1 Continue these patterns by giving the next **three** numbers:
   a) 4 11 18 25 ....
   b) 7 16 25 34 ....
   c) 41 35 29 23 ....
   d) 56 43 30 17 ....

2 Continue these patterns by giving the next **three** numbers:
   a) 5 7 10 14 ....
   b) 7 9 13 19 ....
   c) 32 29 25 20 ....
   d) 100 89 79 70 ....

3 Explain each of the patterns in questions 1 and 2 in words

Remember

Explain sequences using **numbers** to describe the **differences** and **words** like increasing, ascending, decreasing, descending, etc.

Number sequences

Finding missing numbers in a sequence

Look at this sequence:

5   7   9   11   13   15
 ⌣ ⌣ ⌣   ⌣   ⌣
 2   2   2   2   2

Imagine you are given **only the first** and **last** numbers and have to find the missing ones:

5   15

- Find the **difference** between 5 and 15 ... it's 10.
- Now **count the gaps** between the two numbers. There are 5 gaps.
- 10 ÷ 5 = 2 so each number is **2 more than the one before**.

> Fill in the missing numbers in this sequence:
> 4   19

The difference between 4 and 19 is 15 and there are 5 gaps.

15 ÷ 5 = 3, so each number is 3 more than the one before.

Answer: **4 7 10 13 16 19**

> Make sure you count the **number of gaps** and not the number of dotty spaces!

Continuing and explaining number sequences in coordinates

> What patterns can you see in these coordinates?
> (6, 4) (8, 3) (10, 2)

Describe the pattern in the **first** numbers of each pair (the *x* coordinates). Then describe the pattern in the **second** numbers (the *y* coordinates).

Answer: The *x* coordinate **increases by 2** each time.
The *y* coordinate **decreases by 1** each time.

Remember

When filling in numbers missing from a sequence:

- find the **difference**
- count the **gaps**
- **divide** the **difference** by the **number of gaps**.

Test yourself!

1 Fill in the missing numbers in these sequences:

a) 2   22

b) 3   35

c) 24   0

d) 1   21

e) 36   8

2 Fill in the missing numbers in these sequences. You may need to use negative numbers for some:

a) 8   .... −2

b) −3   17

c) 21   .... −19

d) −3   .... −23

e) 32   .... −4

Number sequences

Multiplication sequences

Each multiplication sequence changes because the number is **multiplied** each time.

1 2 4 8 16 32 64 .... (×2)
3 9 27 81 243 .... (×3)
0.0345 3.45 345 .... (×100)

Division sequences

Division sequences change because the number is **divided** each time.

288 144 72 36 18 .... (÷2)
25 000 5000 1000 200 40 .... (÷5)
760 000 76 000 7600 .... (÷10)

Make sure you know how to multiply or divide a number by 10, 100 or 1000. Watch what happens to 54 in the table below. Look at the **direction** the digits move and **how many places** they move by.

	TTh	Th	H	T	U	t	h	tth
(54 × 10) One place to the left			5	4	0.			
(54 × 100) Two places to the left		5	4	0	0.			
(54 × 1000) Three places to the left	5	4	0	0	0.			
54				5	4.			
(54 ÷ 10) One place to the right					5.	4		
(54 ÷ 100) Two places to the right					0.	5	4	
(54 ÷ 1000) Three places to the right					0.	0	5	4

Remember

When **multiplying** by 10, 100 or 1000, the digits move to the **left**. ⟷ When **dividing** by 10, 100 or 1000, the digits move to the **right**.

The decimal point stays where it is, between the units and the tenths!

Number sequences

Following rules

Sometimes you may be asked to continue a number sequence by following a rule, as in the examples below.

The rule is 'Double the last number and add 1'.
Write the next two numbers in the sequence.

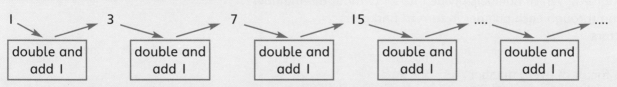

15 → double and add 1 → 31 → double and add 1 → 63

Answer: The next two numbers in the sequence are: **31 63**

The first two numbers are 3.1 and 3.2. The third number is 6.3.
The rule is 'To get the next number, add the two previous numbers'.
Write the next two numbers in the sequence.

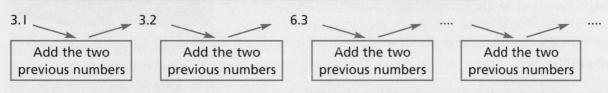

So 3.1 + 3.2 = 6.3 → 3.2 + 6.3 = 9.5 → 6.3 + 9.5 = 15.8

Answer: The sequence continues **9.5 15.8**

Test yourself!

1 Write the missing numbers in these sequences:
   a) The rule is 'Double the last number and add 4'

   5 14 32 ....

   b) The rule is 'Halve the last number and add 10'

   4 12 16 ....

   c) The rule is 'Multiply the last number by 2 and then add 1'

   6 13 27 ....

   d) The rule is 'Find half the last number and add 10'

   36 28 24 ....

   e) The rule is 'Each number is double the previous number'

   .... 3 6 12 24

Remember

Read the rules for the sequences carefully before you begin.

Factors, multiples

Factors

Factors are whole numbers that **divide exactly into another number** without a remainder.

> ### What are the factors of 24?

Ask yourself, 'Which numbers divide into 24 without a remainder?' Then go through each number in turn to find **pairs of factors**.

	Factors of 24	
1 is a factor of every number and so is the number itself (in this case, 24)	1 × 24 = 24	1, 24
2 is a factor as 24 is even	2 × 12 = 24	2, 12
3 is a factor as 3 × 8 is 24	3 × 8 = 24	3, 8
4 is a factor as 4 × 6 is 24	4 × 6 = 24	4, 6
5 is NOT a factor		
6 you already know is a factor.		

Once you reach a number that you already know is a factor, stop!

Answer: **The factors of 24 are** 1, 2, 3, 4, 6, 8, 12 and 24

> You'll need to know your **tables** to help you with factors and multiples. See **page 35** for more tables help and practice.

Multiples

A multiple is a number that is in a **times table or beyond**.

Multiples of **5** are 5, 10, 15, 20, 25, 30 .... and continue (e.g. 85, 115, 500).

The answer to a multiplication question is **a multiple of both the numbers multiplied**. For example, 6 × 7 = 42, so 42 is a multiple of 6 and 7

Multiples of 2, 4, 5, 8 and 10

- Multiples of **2** are **even numbers** (e.g. 18, 34, 530, 416, 2002)
- Multiples of **4** are **even when halved** (e.g. 12, 44, 760, 416, 2004)
- Multiples of **5** **end in 0 or 5** (e.g. 10, 25, 415, 2010)
- Multiples of **8** are **even when halved and halved again** (e.g. 32, 48, 680, 760, 2008) (Half 680 is 340, half 340 is 170. 170 is even, so 680 is a multiple of 8!)
- Multiples of **10** **end in 0** (e.g. 10, 20, 410, 740, 2010).

> ### Test yourself!
>
> 1 How quickly can you answer these?
>
> | | |
> |---|---|
> | 4 × 3 | 6 × 2 |
> | 8 × 3 | 9 × 4 |
> | 4 × 8 | 3 × 7 |
> | 6 × 6 | 7 × 4 |
> | 5 × 9 | 7 × 8 |
>
> 2 Find all the factors of 30 (Clue: there are eight factors)
>
> 3 Find all the factors of 25
>
> 4 Find all the factors of 96
>
> 5 Which of these are multiples of 4?
>   92 740 114 214 242 332
>
> 6 Which of these are multiples of 8?
>   96 240 216 468 242 450

Remember

Factors divide exactly into numbers (e.g. 16 has the **factors** 1, 2, 4, 8 and 16).

Multiples are numbers in your multiplication tables or beyond (e.g. 16 is a **multiple** of 1, 2, 4, 8 and 16).

... and prime numbers

Multiples of 3, 6 and 9

- A number whose **digits** add up to a multiple **of 3** is a multiple of 3, for example:

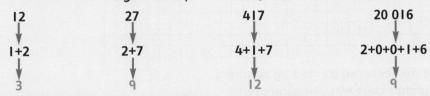

12	27	417	20 016
↓	↓	↓	↓
1+2	2+7	4+1+7	2+0+0+1+6
↓	↓	↓	↓
3	9	12	9

- An **even number** whose **digits** add up to a **multiple of 3** is a multiple of 6 (**e.g.** 18, 42, 108, 31 314)
- A number whose **digits** add up to a **multiple of 9** is a multiple of 9 (**e.g.** 36, 81, 216, 40 725).

Prime numbers

Prime numbers are whole numbers that have only two factors, the **number itself** and 1, like 2, 3, 5, 7, 11, 13, 17, 19, 23, 29, ...

What are the factors of 23?

Ask, 'Which numbers divide into 23 without a remainder?'
The only numbers that divide exactly into 23 without a remainder are 1 and 23.

Answer: 23 is a prime number.

> Apart from the numbers 2 and 5, **all primes end in 1, 3, 7 or 9**.
> So if the number ends in one of these numbers, just use **these tests** to see if it's prime.

Number tests

Learn these simple number tests to see whether a number divides exactly into another without a remainder:

- If a number is **even** it has the factor **2**
- If, when **halved**, the answer is **even**, it has the factor **4**
- If, when **halved and halved again** the answer is **even**, it has the factor **8**
- If a number **ends in 0** it has the factor 10
- If a number **ends in 0 or 5** it has the factor **5**
- If the **digits add up to a** multiple of 3, it has the factor **3**
- If it's **even** and if the **digits add up to a** multiple of 3, it has the factor **6**
- If the **digits add up to a** multiple of 9 it has the factor 9.

Test yourself!

1 Which of these are multiples of 3?
   61 83 178 315 594 613

2 Which of these are multiples of 6?
   56 84 96 284 363 606

3 Which of these are multiples of 9?
   117 186 379 459 702 969

4 Which of these are prime numbers?
   67 69 73 82 91 95 107 473

Remember

Prime numbers have only **two factors**, the number itself and 1.

But ... the number 1 is not prime, because it doesn't have two factors.

Square numbers

Look at this number sequence:

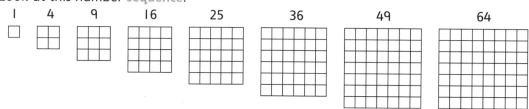

| 1 | 4 | 9 | 16 | 25 | 36 | 49 | 64 |

These are square numbers. Square numbers are created by **squaring** a number (multiplying a whole number by itself). For example:

1^2 (1 squared) = 1 × 1 = 1
2^2 (2 squared) = 2 × 2 = 4
3^2 (3 squared) = 3 × 3 = 9
4^2 (4 squared) = 4 × 4 = 16   These are square numbers.

Square roots

The square root of a number is the number that, when multiplied by itself, gives the first number. (It is the opposite of squaring!)

Examples of square roots

The square root of **16** is **4**, because 4 × 4 = 16
The square root symbol is √ so   √16 = 4
The square root of **36** is **6**, because 6 × 6 = 36
√36 = 6
The square root of **81** is **9**, because 9 × 9 = 81
√81 = 9

You can use the √ key on a calculator to find the square root.

Which number, when multiplied by itself, gives 2209?

Press ⟨2⟩⟨2⟩⟨0⟩⟨9⟩⟨√⟩ to get the answer 47,

because 47 × 47 = 2209

Answer: 47

Square numbers to 100

1	×	1 =	1
2	×	2 =	4
3	×	3 =	9
4	×	4 =	16
5	×	5 =	25
6	×	6 =	36
7	×	7 =	49
8	×	8 =	64
9	×	9 =	81
10	×	10 =	100

Remember

A number **squared** means a number multiplied by itself.

6 squared is written 6^2.
$6^2 = 6 × 6 = 36$
The square root symbol is √
Learn the square numbers to 100! They are listed in the box above.

Test yourself!

1 Cover up the top half of this page. Then write the sequence of the first 12 square numbers

2 Answer these questions without a calculator. Which numbers, multiplied by themselves, give the answer:
   a) 64   b) 121   c) 144

3 Use a calculator to answer these:
   a) which number, multiplied   b) which number, multiplied   c) what is the square
      by itself, gives 1521?   by itself, gives 3249?   root of 1681?

4 Which square number is closest to 5000?

Fractions

A **fraction** is part of something that has been **split into equal parts**.

Fractions are written using two numbers, one on top of the other.

The top number, or numerator,
shows how many of the equal
parts we are talking about.

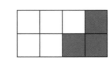

$$\frac{3}{8}$$

The bottom number, or denominator,
shows how many equal parts the
whole has been split into.

Comparing fractions

You can use a fraction wall to help you compare
the sizes of fractions.

Each strip is one whole.

$\frac{1}{2}$ is worth the same as $\frac{2}{4}$.

Another easy way to compare fractions is to make sure
both fractions have the same **denominator**,
like $\frac{3}{7}$ and $\frac{5}{7}$. Then it's easy to see which is larger!

Fraction wall									
One whole									
$\frac{1}{2}$					$\frac{1}{2}$				
$\frac{1}{3}$			$\frac{1}{3}$			$\frac{1}{3}$			
$\frac{1}{4}$		$\frac{1}{4}$		$\frac{1}{4}$			$\frac{1}{4}$		
$\frac{1}{5}$		$\frac{1}{5}$		$\frac{1}{5}$		$\frac{1}{5}$		$\frac{1}{5}$	
$\frac{1}{6}$	$\frac{1}{6}$		$\frac{1}{6}$		$\frac{1}{6}$		$\frac{1}{6}$		$\frac{1}{6}$
$\frac{1}{8}$	$\frac{1}{8}$	$\frac{1}{8}$	$\frac{1}{8}$	$\frac{1}{8}$	$\frac{1}{8}$	$\frac{1}{8}$	$\frac{1}{8}$		
$\frac{1}{10}$	$\frac{1}{10}$	$\frac{1}{10}$	$\frac{1}{10}$	$\frac{1}{10}$	$\frac{1}{10}$	$\frac{1}{10}$	$\frac{1}{10}$	$\frac{1}{10}$	$\frac{1}{10}$

Equivalent fractions

Equivalent fractions stand for the same amount. They can look very
different but are worth the same. Here are some **equivalent fractions**

$$\frac{2}{4}$$

$$\frac{2}{3}$$

$$\frac{1}{2}$$

$$\frac{4}{6}$$

Test yourself!

1 What fractions of these shapes are shaded?

   a)    b)   c)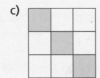

2 Use the fraction wall to compare these fractions. Which is larger:

   a) $\frac{1}{2}$ or $\frac{1}{3}$?

   b) $\frac{1}{3}$ or $\frac{2}{5}$?

   c) $\frac{1}{4}$ or $\frac{2}{10}$?

   d) $\frac{2}{3}$ or $\frac{5}{8}$?

   e) $\frac{5}{8}$ or $\frac{7}{10}$?

Remember

Equivalent fractions can
look very different but are
worth the same.

Fractions

Recognising equivalent fractions

If you can multiply or divide the numerator **and** the denominator by the **same number** to make the other fraction, then both fractions are **equivalent** ...

> **Examples of equivalent fractions**
>
> $\dfrac{2}{3}$ ⤵⤴ $\dfrac{4}{6}$ ×2 ×2
>
> $\dfrac{12}{15}$ ⤵⤴ $\dfrac{4}{5}$ ÷3 ÷3

Finding an equivalent fraction

To find an equivalent fraction you can multiply or divide the **numerator** and the **denominator** of a fraction by any number you choose. The new fraction will be equivalent!

> **How to find an equivalent fraction**
>
> ×5 $\dfrac{1}{6}$ ⤵⤴ $\dfrac{5}{30}$ ×5
>
> ÷4 $\dfrac{20}{24}$ ⤵⤴ $\dfrac{5}{6}$ ÷4
>
> ÷100 $\dfrac{300}{500}$ ⤵⤴ $\dfrac{3}{5}$ ÷100

Cancelling a fraction to its simplest (or lowest) form

When we divide the numerator and the denominator by the largest number we can, and can't divide again by any other number, we say we have cancelled the fraction to its **simplest (or lowest) form**.

> **Cancel these fractions to their simplest form**
>
> ÷4 $\dfrac{4}{28}$ ⤵⤴ $\dfrac{1}{7}$ ÷4
>
> ÷10 $\dfrac{50}{70}$ ⤵⤴ $\dfrac{5}{7}$ ÷10
>
> ÷3 $\dfrac{30}{51}$ ⤵⤴ $\dfrac{10}{17}$ ÷3

You might be asked to give some fractions that are equivalent to another fraction, like this ...

> **Give three fractions equivalent to $\dfrac{3}{5}$**
>
> ×2 $\dfrac{3}{5}$ ⤵⤴ $\dfrac{6}{10}$ ×2
>
> ×3 $\dfrac{3}{5}$ ⤵⤴ $\dfrac{9}{15}$ ×3
>
> ×10 $\dfrac{3}{5}$ ⤵⤴ $\dfrac{30}{50}$ ×10

Test yourself!

1 Which of these pairs of fractions are equivalent?

  a) $\dfrac{3}{5}$ and $\dfrac{9}{15}$

  b) $\dfrac{3}{5}$ and $\dfrac{12}{16}$

  c) $\dfrac{3}{8}$ and $\dfrac{9}{24}$

  d) $\dfrac{15}{18}$ and $\dfrac{5}{6}$

  e) $\dfrac{12}{20}$ and $\dfrac{3}{5}$

2 Cancel these fractions to their simplest form:

  a) $\dfrac{6}{24}$

  b) $\dfrac{15}{18}$

  c) $\dfrac{9}{33}$

  d) $\dfrac{8}{22}$

  e) $\dfrac{20}{28}$

3 Give three fractions equivalent to:

  a) $\dfrac{3}{4}$

  b) $\dfrac{30}{40}$

  c) $\dfrac{4}{5}$

  d) $\dfrac{100}{500}$

  e) $\dfrac{2}{3}$

Remember

If you can multiply the **numerator** and the **denominator** by the **same number** to make the other fraction, then both fractions are equivalent.

Fractions

Mixed numbers

A **mixed number**, like $4\frac{1}{2}$, contains a **whole number (4)** and a **fraction** ($\frac{1}{2}$).

Improper fractions

An **improper fraction** is sometimes called a 'top-heavy' fraction because the numerator (top number) is larger than the denominator. Improper fractions are worth more than one whole. For example, $\frac{5}{2}$, $\frac{7}{3}$, $\frac{9}{6}$ and $\frac{10}{2}$ are improper fractions.

Changing a mixed number to an improper fraction

Change $5\frac{3}{4}$ to an improper fraction

There are four quarters in a whole one and we have five whole ones, so that's 20 quarters. Add on the other three quarters. That makes $\frac{23}{4}$. $5\frac{3}{4}$ is $\frac{23}{4}$.

Answer: $\frac{23}{4}$

A quick way is to say, '4 times 5 equals 20, add 3, equals 23'.

Changing an improper fraction to a mixed number

Change $\frac{23}{4}$ to a mixed number

There are four quarters in a whole one and we have 23 quarters, so that's five whole ones and three quarters left over. That makes $5\frac{3}{4}$. $\frac{23}{4}$ is $5\frac{3}{4}$.

Answer: $5\frac{3}{4}$

A quick way is to say, '23 divided by 4 is 5 and 3 left over'.

Test yourself!

1 Change these mixed numbers to improper fractions:

a) $3\frac{1}{2}$

b) $5\frac{1}{2}$

c) $2\frac{1}{4}$

d) $4\frac{3}{4}$

e) $5\frac{1}{3}$

f) $7\frac{2}{3}$

g) $6\frac{3}{5}$

h) $5\frac{2}{5}$

2 Change these improper fractions to mixed numbers:

a) $\frac{8}{3}$

b) $\frac{9}{4}$

c) $\frac{15}{2}$

d) $\frac{21}{4}$

e) $\frac{16}{5}$

f) $\frac{18}{8}$

g) $\frac{22}{5}$

h) $\frac{37}{10}$

Remember

Mixed numbers contain a whole number and a fraction.

Improper fractions have a **numerator** larger than the **denominator** – they are top heavy!

Fractions

Finding fractions of an amount in your head

Fractions with a numerator (top number) of 1 (e.g. $\frac{1}{2}, \frac{1}{5}, \frac{1}{6}, \frac{1}{10}$) are called **unit fractions**. Find a unit fraction by dividing the number by the denominator (bottom number).

Finding a unit fraction of a number

$\frac{1}{5}$ of 45 = 45 ÷ **5 = 9**

$\frac{1}{8}$ of 56 = 56 ÷ **8 = 7**

Once you can find a **unit fraction** you can find **any** fraction of a number **by multiplying**.

Finding any fraction of a number

$\frac{2}{5}$ of 45   45 ÷ 5 = 9,   9 × 2 = **18**

↗ one fifth   ↖ two-fifths

$\frac{5}{8}$ of 56   56 ÷ 8 = 7   7 × 5 = **35**

↗ one eighth   ↖ five-eighths

Finding fractions of amounts with a calculator

You can also find fractions using **a calculator**. Divide by the denominator and multiply by the numerator, as before. To check whether you divided and multiplied correctly, see if your answer looks 'about right'.

Find $\frac{5}{9}$ of £108

Key in **108 ÷ 9 × 5**, which gives **60**.

Answer: £60

Check: $\frac{5}{9}$ is a bit more than $\frac{1}{2}$, so $\frac{5}{9}$ of £108 should be a bit more than half of £108. £60 is about right. If you had got it the wrong way round, the answer would have been larger than £108!

Remember

To find **unit fractions**: **divide** by the **denominator**. To find other fractions: find the **unit fraction and** then **multiply** by the **numerator**.

Test yourself!

1 Find these unit fractions:
   a) $\frac{1}{4}$ of 24
   b) $\frac{1}{3}$ of 18
   c) $\frac{1}{5}$ of 35
   d) $\frac{1}{6}$ of 42
   e) $\frac{1}{7}$ of 42
   f) $\frac{1}{8}$ of 32

2 Find these fractions without using a calculator:
   a) $\frac{3}{4}$ of 32
   b) $\frac{2}{3}$ of 24
   c) $\frac{3}{5}$ of 40
   d) $\frac{5}{6}$ of £48
   e) $\frac{3}{7}$ of £21
   f) $\frac{5}{8}$ of 48kg

3 Use a calculator to find these fractions:
   a) $\frac{4}{7}$ of 56
   b) $\frac{5}{8}$ of 128
   c) $\frac{3}{5}$ of 105kg
   d) $\frac{7}{9}$ of 135cm
   e) $\frac{6}{7}$ of £91
   f) $\frac{7}{8}$ of 192m

Decimals

Decimals, like fractions, are part numbers. They show us numbers that aren't whole, e.g., 0.1, 3.54 and 102.629

It is important to know what each digit in a decimal number stands for ...

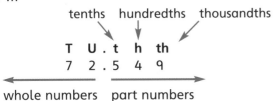

tenths   hundredths   thousandths

T U . t h th
7 2 . 5 4 9

whole numbers   part numbers

The numbers to the left of the decimal point show how many whole numbers we have. The numbers to the right show us how many tenths, hundredths, thousandths etc. we have.

Equivalence of fractions and decimals

A tenth, or 0.1, is the same as the fraction $\frac{1}{10}$

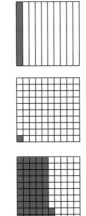

A hundredth, or 0.01, is the same as $\frac{1}{100}$ and so on.

So 0.52 means 5 tenths and 2 hundredths $\frac{52}{100}$ or 52 hundredths

---

Change 0.37 to a fraction

0.37 means 3 tenths and 7 hundredths or **37 hundredths.**

Write 37 hundredths as a fraction.

Answer: $\frac{37}{100}$

Change $\frac{63}{100}$ to a decimal

$\frac{63}{100}$ (63 hundredths) is the same as 0.63.

Answer: **0.63**

Test yourself!

1 Write these decimals as fractions:
   a) 0.3
   b) 0.9
   c) 0.54
   d) 0.78
   e) 0.391

2 Write these fractions as decimals:
   a) $\frac{2}{10}$
   b) $\frac{8}{10}$
   c) $\frac{40}{100}$
   d) $\frac{78}{100}$
   e) $\frac{400}{1000}$

The dot that separates the whole numbers from the part numbers is called the decimal point.

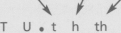

5.9 6

Remember

tenths hundredths thousandths

T U . t h th

0.1   = 1 tenth = $\frac{1}{10}$

0.01   = 1 hundredth = $\frac{1}{100}$

0.001 = 1 thousandth = $\frac{1}{1000}$

Decimals

Ordering decimals

Ordering decimals is like ordering whole numbers (see page 8).
Begin by comparing the left-hand digits. If they are the same, move
to the right to compare the next digits, etc.

Put these decimals in order of size, largest first:
0.783   0.88   0.78   0.9   0.792

Which number has most tenths? ⟶ 0.9
Which has the next greatest number of tenths? ⟶ 0.88
Which numbers have the next greatest number of tenths?
  0.7832   0.70   0.792
Which of these has most hundredths? ⟶ 0.792
Which numbers have the next greatest number of hundredths?
  0.783   0.78
Which of these has more thousandths? ⟶ 0.783
Which is the smallest number? ⟶ 0.78

Answer: 0.9   0.88   0.792   0.783   0.78

Useful tip!

Some people put extra zeros on the end of the decimals so that
each decimal has the same number of digits:

  0.783   0.880   0.780   0.900   0.792

This doesn't **change** the numbers, 0.9 = 0.90 = 0.900 etc.,
but it makes them **easier to compare**, e.g.:

  0.900 is larger than **0.783**

So the correct order is:

  0.900   0.880   0.792   0.783   0.780

Remember

When ordering, put **extra zeros** on the end of the decimals so
each has **the same number of digits**.

Test yourself!

1 Which is the larger
   decimal in each pair?
   a) 0.8, 0.79

   b) 0.37, 0.34

   c) 3.658, 3.7

2 Put these decimals in
   order of size, smallest
   first:
   a) 0.5, 0.8, 0.7, 0.75, 0.62

   b) 0.6, 0.65, 0.73, 0.64,
      0.72

   c) 2.28, 2.31, 2.304, 2.3,
      2.296

   d) 3.524, 3.56, 3.52, 3.563,
      3.6

   e) 0.876, 0.867, 0.687,
      0.678, 0.768

For more on ordering,
see page 8.

Decimals

Decimals on a number line

Decimals lie between whole numbers and can be shown by zooming in on a number line.

This line shows tenths between 15 and 16:

This line shows hundredths between 15.4 and 15.5:

This line shows hundredths between 15.44 and 15.45:

Rounding decimals

Round 0.67 to the nearest tenth

One way of rounding is draw a number line and see which tenth the number is nearest to.

0.6   0.67   0.7

It is nearer to 0.7

Answer: **0.7**

Here is a second way of rounding …

1 See what you are rounding to.
   Round 0.67 **to the nearest tenth**

2 Point to this digit in the number …
   U . t h
   0.6 7

3 Look at the digit to the right of it …
   0.6 7

4 If it's smaller than 5, your digit stays the same.
   If it's 5 or larger, your digit goes up one.

   0 . 7

Answer: **0.7**

For more on rounding,
see pages 6 and 7.

Test yourself!

1 Draw a number line with 10 intervals, showing the decimals between 12 and 13

2 Draw a number line with 10 intervals, showing the decimals between 8.5 and 8.6

3 Round these decimals to the nearest tenth:
   a) 0.84

   b) 0.37

   c) 4.56

   d) 0.85

   e) 0.492

Remember

Putting zeros on the end of decimals doesn't change them

15.5 is the same as 15.50

15.4 15.41 15.42 15.43 15.44 15.45 15.46 15.47 15.48 15.49 15.5

Percentages

Percentages, like fractions and decimals, can be used to show parts of a whole. A percentage is a fraction with a denominator of 100, but written in a different way. 36% means $\frac{36}{100}$. Per cent means 'out of a hundred'. Thirty-six per cent is '36 out of 100'.

Percentages, fractions and decimals

Percentages, fractions and decimals like these all have the same value:

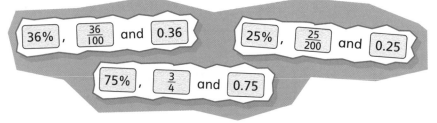

36%, $\frac{36}{100}$ and 0.36   25%, $\frac{25}{200}$ and 0.25   75%, $\frac{3}{4}$ and 0.75

The fraction $\frac{75}{100}$ has been changed to its simplest form, $\frac{3}{4}$ (see page 20).

We can place them all on a number line, as in the example below.

Write 60% as a decimal and as a fraction in its simplest form

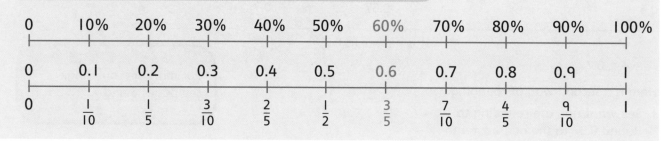

0	10%	20%	30%	40%	50%	60%	70%	80%	90%	100%
0	0.1	0.2	0.3	0.4	0.5	0.6	0.7	0.8	0.9	1
0	$\frac{1}{10}$	$\frac{1}{5}$	$\frac{3}{10}$	$\frac{2}{5}$	$\frac{1}{2}$	$\frac{3}{5}$	$\frac{7}{10}$	$\frac{4}{5}$	$\frac{9}{10}$	1

Converting percentages to decimals

To convert a percentage to a decimal, **divide** by 100.

36% → 36 ÷ 100 = 0.36
75% → 75 ÷ 100 = 0.75

Converting decimals to percentages

To convert a decimal to a percentage, **multiply** by 100.

0.7 → 0.7 × 100 = 70%
0.38 → 0.38 × 100 = 38%

Remember

Always think of the % sign as 'out of 100' or 'divided by 100'.
A **percentage** is a fraction with a **denominator** of 100.

Percentages

Converting percentages to fractions

To convert a percentage to a fraction, write the percentage as a fraction with a denominator of 100. Then divide the numerator and denominator by the same number to find the simplest form.

Convert 36% to a fraction

$36\% = \frac{36}{100}$

$$\frac{36}{100} \xrightarrow[\div 4]{\div 4} \frac{9}{25}$$

Answer: $\frac{9}{25}$

Converting fractions to percentages

To convert a fraction to a percentage, multiply the numerator and denominator by the same number to give a denominator of 100.

Convert $\frac{11}{20}$ into a fraction with a denominator of 100

$$\frac{11}{20} \xrightarrow[\times 5]{\times 5} \frac{?}{100} = \frac{55}{100}$$ (This is the same as **55%**)

Remember

50% is $\frac{1}{2}$ Halve the number.

25% is $\frac{1}{4}$ Halve and halve again.

75% is $\frac{3}{4}$ Halve and halve again and add the two answers.

Finding easy percentages in your head

There are several ways to find a percentage of a number or amount.

Remember that   50% is $\frac{1}{2}$,   25% is $\frac{1}{4}$ and 75% is $\frac{3}{4}$

To find 50%: halve the number

50% of £480   half of £480 = £240

To find 25%: halve the number and halve the answer
(or just divide by 4)

25% of £480   **half** of £480 = £240, **half** of £240 = £120

To find 75%: halve the number and halve the answer,
then add your two answers together

75% of £480   **half** of £480 = £240, **half** of £240 = £120, £240 + £120 = £360

Percentages

Finding other percentages in your head

To find other percentages in your head, you can use this scale divided into 10% sections:

0	10%	20%	30%	40%	50%	60%	70%	80%	90%	100%
0	$\frac{1}{10}$	$\frac{2}{10}$	$\frac{3}{10}$	$\frac{4}{10}$	$\frac{1}{2}$	$\frac{6}{10}$	$\frac{7}{10}$	$\frac{8}{10}$	$\frac{9}{10}$	1

To find 10%: divide the number by 10

10% of 800 ⟶ 800 ÷ 10 = 80

10% of £480 ⟶ £480 ÷ 10 = £48

To find 20%: divide by 10 and double

20% of 800 ⟶ 800 ÷ 10 = 80, 80 × 2 = 160

20% of £480 ⟶ £480 ÷ 10 = £48 £48 × 2 = £96

To find 30%: divide by 10 and multiply by 3

30% of 800 ⟶ 800 ÷ 10 = 80, 80 × 3 = 240

30% of £480 ⟶ £480 ÷ 10 = £48 £48 × 3 = £144

To find 40%: divide by 10 and multiply by 4, etc.

For **all percentages that are multiples of 10**, use your answer to 10% to help you.

Solving percentage problems

In a sale, you pay 60% of the normal price. The normal price for a jacket is £40.

How much is the sale price?

To find 60% of £40, find 10% of £40 (£4) and then multiply by 6

Answer: £24

A woman spends 30% of her earnings on petrol. She earns £24 000 in a year.

How much does she spend on petrol?

To find 30% of £24 000, find 10% of £24 000 (£2400) and then multiply by 3

Answer: £7200

Test yourself!

1   Find 10% of these amounts:
   a) £120
   b) 450kg
   c) 1270m
   d) 254km

2   Find 30% of these amounts:
   a) £250
   b) 400kg
   c) 160cm
   d) 240m

3   Find 70% of these amounts:
   a) £80
   b) 90kg
   c) 110cm
   d) 250m

4   Solve this problem:
   I have £260 in my bank account. I earn 5% interest on this money.
   How much interest do I earn?

Remember

For all percentages that are multiples of 10, use your answer to 10% to help you find percentages of amounts.

Percentages

Finding percentages on a calculator

Some calculators have a percentage key (see page 41). However, there are two other ways of finding percentages using a calculator.

Using fractions

A percentage can be written as a fraction with a **denominator** of 100.

> Find 68% of £132
>
> Here, the word '**of**' means '**multiply**'.
> To find **68% of £132**, enter 68% as a **fraction**.
>
> $\frac{68}{100} \times £132 = £89.76$ ⟵ Enter 68 ÷ 100 and then × 132
>
> Answer: £89.76

Using decimals

We can also write a percentage as a **decimal** (see page 26).

> Find 68% of £132
>
> To find **68% of £132**, enter 68% as a **decimal**.
>
> $0.68 \times £132 = £89.76$
>
> Answer: £89.76
>
> Always check your answer,
> **68%** is a bit more than two thirds
>
> 68% of £132 = £89.76 ⟶
>
> **check**
> $\frac{1}{3}$ of £132 is about £40
> $\frac{2}{3}$ of £132 is about £80
> £89.76 is a bit more than £80
> So it is probably right.

Test yourself!

1 Use a calculator to find these percentages:
  a) 18% of 66
  b) 36% of 92
  c) 46% of £70
  d) 78% of £64
  e) 99% of 137kg
  f) 47% of 83kg
  g) 88% of 570m
  h) 95% of 1345

2 Solve these problems:
  a) A puppy weighs 64% of its expected weight. Its expected weight was 95 ounces. How much does it weigh?
  b) A train travels at 72mph. It slows down to 45% of that speed. How fast is it travelling now?
  c) A garage adds 17.5% VAT to the cost of a repair. How much is the VAT for a repair costing £162?

Remember

Use the multiplication sign in place of the word 'of'.

Summary

Fractions, decimals and percentages are different ways of saying the same thing.
This diagram summarises how to change between them:

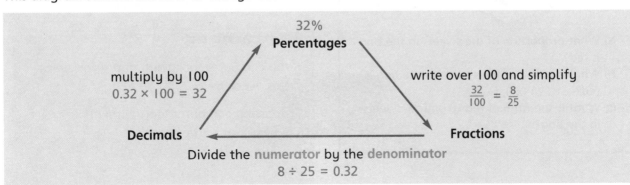

32%
Percentages

multiply by 100
0.32 × 100 = 32

write over 100 and simplify
$\frac{32}{100} = \frac{8}{25}$

Decimals

Fractions

Divide the numerator by the denominator
8 ÷ 25 = 0.32

Ratio and proportion

We use ratio and proportion to compare numbers or quantities.

Ratio is the relationship between two or more quantities. It compares 'part with part'.
Compare **the red parts with the white parts** of this rod.
There are 3 reds **for every** I white part. So the **ratio** of red to white is **3 to 1**, written 3:1.

Proportion is the relationship between part of something and the whole thing. It compares 'part with whole'.
This time, compare **the red parts of the rod with the whole rod**.
3 **in every** 4 parts are red. So the **proportion** of red parts is **3 out of 4**. Think of proportion as a fraction: the fraction that is red is $\frac{3}{4}$. We can also write this proportion as **0.75 or 75%**.

Using ratio and proportion

Use ratio to compare the numbers of red and yellow squares in this shape.
There are 6 red and 3 yellow.
The **ratio** is 6 to 3 (6:3), simplified to 2:1.

Use proportion to compare the number of red squares with the total number.
There are 6 red squares out of a total of 9.
The **proportion** is 6 out of 9 ($\frac{6}{9}$), simplified to $\frac{2}{3}$.

Test yourself!

1 Look at the squares in this shape:

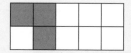

a) What proportion of the squares is red?
b) What fraction of the squares is red?
c) What is the ratio of red to white squares?

2 Look at the bag of sweets:

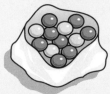

a) What proportion of the sweets in the bag is red?
b) What fraction of the sweets in the bag is red?
c) What is the ratio of red to yellow sweets in the bag?

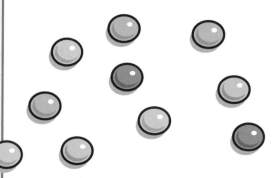

Remember

Ratio compares 'part with part' ('**for every**' or '**to every**').

Proportion compares 'part with whole' ('**in every**' or '**out of every**').

Ratio and proportion problems

In the drawing below ... How many black CDs to silver CDs are there?
What fraction of all the CDs is black?

Answer: Black CDs to silver CDs (ratio): 5:3
The fraction of CDs that is black (proportion): $\frac{5}{8}$

Rob has 4 CDs for every 1 that Jo has. Rob has 12 CDs.
How many has Jo?

Write pairs of numbers in the ratio of 4:1.

Rob	Jo
4	1
8	2
12	3

Answer: Jo has 3 CDs.

Dev makes soup using 3 mushrooms for every 2 tomatoes.
He uses 15 mushrooms. How many tomatoes does he use?

Write pairs of numbers in the ratio 3:2.

mushrooms	tomatoes
3	2
6	4
9	6
12	8
15	10

Answer: 10 tomatoes.

There are 32 pupils in a class in the ratio 3 boys to every
5 girls, or 3:5. How many boys are there?

Find the proportion of boys in the class by adding the numbers
in the ratio.

3 boys + 5 girls = 8 pupils. 3 out of 8 pupils are boys ($\frac{3}{8}$).

Find $\frac{3}{8}$ of 32. Find $\frac{1}{8}$ by dividing 32 by 8 ... 32 ÷ 8 = 4.

If $\frac{1}{8}$ is 4, then $\frac{3}{8}$ is 4 × 3 = 12.

So 12 out of 32 pupils are boys.

Answer: 12

Test yourself!

1 Peter shares out 15 sweets.
   He gives Kate 1 for every
   4 he eats.
   How many does Kate get?

2 At the tennis club there
   are 2 boys for every 3 girls.
   There are 20 children
   altogether.
   How many are boys?

3 There are 4 toffees to
   every 3 chocolates in a bag
   of 28 sweets.
   How many toffees are
   there?

4 Sam mixes 2 tins of blue
   paint with 1 tin of white.
   He uses 12 tins of paint
   altogether.
   How many tins are blue?

Remember

Always change ratios to
their simplest form, as with
equivalent fractions, e.g.

- 9:6 ⟶ 3:2
- 15:3 ⟶ 5:1
- 12:28 ⟶ 3:7

Mental addition and subtraction

Adding and subtracting 10 and 100

To add or subtract **10**, add or subtract **1** to or from the digit in the **tens** column:

529 + 10 = 539   529 − 10 = 519

To add or subtract **100**, add or subtract **1** to or from the digit in the **hundreds** column:

1467 + 100 = 1567   1467 − 100 = 1367

Adding or subtracting near multiples of 10

To add or subtract numbers close to a multiple of 10 (e.g. 49 or 58), add or subtract the multiple of 10 and **adjust afterwards**, as in the example below.

39 + 54 ➤ 40 + 54 = 94 ➤ subtract 1 ➤ 93

76 − 48 ➤ 76 − 50 = 26 ➤ add 2 ➤ 28

Use the same method to add and subtract numbers that are close to multiples of 100, as in the next example. Always check whether you need to adjust by adding or subtracting!

574 + 97 ➤ 574 + 100 = 674 ➤ subtract 3 ➤ 671

837 − 198 ➤ 837 − 200 = 637 ➤ add 2 ➤ 639

Using blank number lines

When counting up or back through 10, 100, 1000 etc., use blank number lines.

Find the difference between 705 and 687

Draw a line with 687 at the left end and 705 at the right.

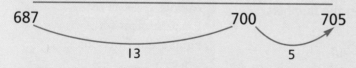

687   700   705
        13   5

Write 700 on the line. Count from 687 to 700 and then on to 705. Add 13 + 5 = 18.
Answer: 18

Test yourself!

1 Add 10 to these numbers:
a) 94
b) 392
c) 996

2 Subtract 10 from these numbers:
a) 107
b) 701
c) 1005

3 Add or subtract these numbers:
a) 49 + 26
b) 134 + 58
c) 78 − 49
d) 354 − 151

4 Find the difference between:
a) 703 and 689
b) 608 and 591
c) 786 and 808
d) 1294 and 1307
e) 2609 and 2578

Written addition

Addition

When numbers get too large to work with in your head, you need another method. When adding numbers on paper, make sure you **line the columns up** correctly and **approximate first**.

565 + 234

Approximation: 600 + 200 = 800

H	T	U	
5	6	5	
+ 2	3	4	This calculation has no carrying.
7	9	9	

Answer: 799

Test yourself!

1 Approximate first then add these numbers:
   a) 431 + 56
   b) 730 + 284
   c) 658 + 297
   d) 1739 + 2047
   e) 3917 + 5009

2 Approximate first then add these decimal numbers:
   a) 21.5 + 16.4
   b) 36.8 + 27.1
   c) 57.92 + 6.8
   d) 87.19 + 16.8
   e) 152.87 + 305.74

7538 + 26 904

Approximation: 8000 + 27 000 = 35 000

TTh	Th	H	T	U
	7	5	3	8
+ 2	6	9	0	4
3	4	4	4	2
1	1		1	

0 + 2 + 1 = 3, write 3 in the ten thousands column	7 + 6 + 1 = 14, write 4 and carry 1 ten thousand	5 + 9 = 14, write 4 and carry 1 thousand into the thousands column	3 + 0 + 1 = 4, write 4 in the tens column	8 + 4 = 12, write 2 and carry 1 ten into the tens column

This calculation has lots of carrying!
Follow the boxes if you're not sure.

Answer: 34 442

Adding decimals

Add decimals in the same way as whole numbers. Just be careful to **line up each column** and each decimal point **correctly**.

36.3 + 52.86

Approximation: 36 + 53 = 89

T	U	.	t	h	
3	6	.	3	0	← put a 0 here
+ 5	2	.	8	6	
8	9	.	1	6	
			1		

Answer: 89.16

Remember

When adding decimals, line up the decimal points. The decimal point separates whole numbers from 'part numbers'.

Written subtraction

Subtraction

When subtracting large numbers, make sure you **line the columns up correctly** and **approximate first**. Watch out for when you need to **exchange**.

647 – 432

Approximation: 600 – 400 = 200

```
  H   T   U
  6   4   7
– 4   3   2
  2   1   5
```

Answer: 215

This calculation has no exchange.
Check your answer by **adding** the last two rows:
432 + 215 = 647

Remember

When subtracting decimals, line up the decimal points.

7632 – 2815

Approximation: 8000 – 3000 = 5000

```
   Th            H            T           U
   7̶ 6          ¹6          3̶ 2         ¹2
 –  2            8            1           5
   4            8            1           7
```

| 6 – 2 = 4, write 4. | 6 – 8 we can't do, so borrow one thousand and change it into 10 hundreds. Cross out 1 of the thousands. Take 8 from 16. Write 8. | 2 –1 = 1. Write 1 in the tens column. | 2 – 5 we can't do, so borrow one ten and change it into 10 units. Cross out 1 of the tens. The 2 becomes 12. Take 5 from 12. Write 7. |

This calculation needs exchanges. Follow the boxes if you're not sure.

Answer: 4817

Subtracting decimals

Subtract decimals in the same way as whole numbers. Just be careful to line up each column and each decimal point correctly.

52.97 – 36.8

Approximation: 53 – 37 = 16

```
  T   U  .  t   h
  5̶ 4  ¹2 .  9   7
– 3   6  .  8   0   ◄— put a 0 here
  1   6  .  1   7
```

Answer: 16.17

1 Approximate first, then subtract these numbers:
   a) 685 – 43
   b) 629 – 283
   c) 548 – 339
   d) 2794 – 1697
   e) 3408 – 2619

2 Approximate first, then subtract these decimals:
   a) 32.5 – 21.4
   b) 56.9 – 27.3
   c) 41.92 – 17.86
   d) 76.15 – 38.26
   e) 540.31 – 406.54

Multiplication facts

Learning tables

Learn these tables facts and remember – if you know one fact you can just turn it around to get another. It's two for the price of one! For example,

$7 \times 9 = 63$ **and** $9 \times 7 = 63$

Multiplication tables

3×	4×	6×	7×	8×	9×
$3 \times 0 = 0$	$4 \times 0 = 0$	$6 \times 0 = 0$	$7 \times 0 = 0$	$8 \times 0 = 0$	$9 \times 0 = 0$
$3 \times 1 = 3$	$4 \times 1 = 4$	$6 \times 1 = 6$	$7 \times 1 = 7$	$8 \times 1 = 8$	$9 \times 1 = 9$
$3 \times 2 = 6$	$4 \times 2 = 8$	$6 \times 2 = 12$	$7 \times 2 = 14$	$8 \times 2 = 16$	$9 \times 2 = 18$
$3 \times 3 = 9$	$4 \times 3 = 12$	$6 \times 3 = 18$	$7 \times 3 = 21$	$8 \times 3 = 24$	$9 \times 3 = 27$
$3 \times 4 = 12$	$4 \times 4 = 16$	$6 \times 4 = 24$	$7 \times 4 = 28$	$8 \times 4 = 32$	$9 \times 4 = 36$
$3 \times 5 = 15$	$4 \times 5 = 20$	$6 \times 5 = 30$	$7 \times 5 = 35$	$8 \times 5 = 40$	$9 \times 5 = 45$
$3 \times 6 = 18$	$4 \times 6 = 24$	$6 \times 6 = 36$	$7 \times 6 = 42$	$8 \times 6 = 48$	$9 \times 6 = 54$
$3 \times 7 = 21$	$4 \times 7 = 28$	$6 \times 7 = 42$	$7 \times 7 = 49$	$8 \times 7 = 56$	$9 \times 7 = 63$
$3 \times 8 = 24$	$4 \times 8 = 32$	$6 \times 8 = 48$	$7 \times 8 = 56$	$8 \times 8 = 64$	$9 \times 8 = 72$
$3 \times 9 = 27$	$4 \times 9 = 36$	$6 \times 9 = 54$	$7 \times 9 = 63$	$8 \times 9 = 72$	$9 \times 9 = 81$
$3 \times 10 = 30$	$4 \times 10 = 40$	$6 \times 10 = 60$	$7 \times 10 = 70$	$8 \times 10 = 80$	$9 \times 10 = 90$

Tips to help you learn your tables

- Write down **one fact a day** and stick it somewhere you will see it often – beside the TV or on the fridge!

- **Use facts you know:**
  if you know $7 \times 6 = 42$ then 8×6 is 6 more than 42.

- As soon as you learn a fact **turn it round to** learn the other: if you know $9 \times 6 = 54$ then you know $6 \times 9 = 54$.

Remember

If you know one tables fact, just turn it around to get another.

Test yourself!

1 Cover up the tables grid and try these:

8×5	5×8
3×6	6×3
4×5	5×4
7×3	3×7
6×8	8×6
9×4	4×9
4×8	8×4
9×7	7×9
8×9	9×8
3×9	9×3
9×5	5×9
7×8	8×7
6×7	7×6
6×9	9×6
7×7	3×3
4×4	6×6
8×8	9×9

Division facts

Once you know your **multiplication tables**, **division** becomes easier too. If you know a tables fact, you automatically know two division facts. For example,

7 × 9 = 63

63 ÷ 9 = 7 and **63 ÷ 7 = 9**

Division tables

÷ 3	÷ 4	÷ 6	÷ 7	÷ 8	÷ 9
3 ÷ 3 = 1	4 ÷ 4 = 1	6 ÷ 6 = 1	7 ÷ 7 = 1	8 ÷ 8 = 1	9 ÷ 9 = 1
6 ÷ 3 = 2	8 ÷ 4 = 2	12 ÷ 6 = 2	14 ÷ 7 = 2	16 ÷ 8 = 2	18 ÷ 9 = 2
9 ÷ 3 = 3	12 ÷ 4 = 3	18 ÷ 6 = 3	21 ÷ 7 = 3	24 ÷ 8 = 3	27 ÷ 9 = 3
12 ÷ 3 = 4	16 ÷ 4 = 4	24 ÷ 6 = 4	28 ÷ 7 = 4	32 ÷ 8 = 4	36 ÷ 9 = 4
15 ÷ 3 = 5	20 ÷ 4 = 5	30 ÷ 6 = 5	35 ÷ 7 = 5	40 ÷ 8 = 5	45 ÷ 9 = 5
18 ÷ 3 = 6	24 ÷ 4 = 6	36 ÷ 6 = 6	42 ÷ 7 = 6	48 ÷ 8 = 6	54 ÷ 9 = 6
21 ÷ 3 = 7	28 ÷ 4 = 7	42 ÷ 6 = 7	49 ÷ 7 = 7	56 ÷ 8 = 7	63 ÷ 9 = 7
24 ÷ 3 = 8	32 ÷ 4 = 8	48 ÷ 6 = 8	56 ÷ 7 = 8	64 ÷ 8 = 8	72 ÷ 9 = 8
27 ÷ 3 = 9	36 ÷ 4 = 9	54 ÷ 6 = 9	63 ÷ 7 = 9	72 ÷ 8 = 9	81 ÷ 9 = 9
30 ÷ 3 = 10	40 ÷ 4 = 10	60 ÷ 6 = 10	70 ÷ 7 = 10	80 ÷ 8 = 10	90 ÷ 9 = 10

Tips to help you learn division facts

• Write down one fact a day and stick it somewhere you will see it often – by the bathroom mirror or opposite the toilet!

• Use the multiplication facts you know:
if you know 8 × 9 = 72 then you know another multiplication fact, 9 × 8 = 72 **and** you know two division facts 72 ÷ 8 = 9 and 72 ÷ 9 = 8.

• Remove the picture cards from a pack of playing cards. Shuffle them and turn them face down. Turn two over at a time. Multiply them and then write down both division facts.

Remember

If you know a tables fact, you automatically know two division facts.

Test yourself!

1 Cover up the tables grid and try these:

40 ÷ 5	40 ÷ 8
18 ÷ 6	18 ÷ 3
20 ÷ 5	20 ÷ 4
21 ÷ 3	21 ÷ 7
48 ÷ 8	48 ÷ 6
36 ÷ 4	36 ÷ 9
32 ÷ 8	32 ÷ 4
63 ÷ 7	63 ÷ 9
72 ÷ 9	72 ÷ 8
27 ÷ 9	27 ÷ 3
45 ÷ 5	45 ÷ 9
56 ÷ 8	56 ÷ 7
42 ÷ 7	42 ÷ 6
54 ÷ 9	54 ÷ 6
49 ÷ 7	9 ÷ 3
16 ÷ 4	36 ÷ 6
64 ÷ 8	81 ÷ 9

Mental multiplication

Multiplying by 10

To **multiply by 10**, move each digit **one place** to the **left**.

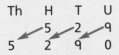

Th	H	T	U
	5	2	9
5	2	9	0

Answer: **5290**

Multiplying by 100

To **multiply by 100**, move each digit **two places** to the **left**.

529 × 100

TTh	Th	H	T	U
		5	2	9
5	2	9	0	0

Answer: **52900**

Doubling

Doubling can help you to multiply numbers.
To multiply a number:

- by 2 – just double it
- by 4 – double and double again
- by 8 – double, double and double again

34 × 2 double 34 = **68**
16 × 4 double 16 = 32,
　　　　double 32 = **64**
19 × 8 double 19 = 38,
　　　　double 38 = 76,
　　　　double 76 = **152**

Using factors

Using factors (see page 16) can make multiplying in your head easier. Look at the example below.

25 × 18

6 and 3 are **factors** of 18, so we can break 18 into 6 × 3, and the question become: 25 × 6 × 3
25 × 6 = 150 and 150 × 3 = 450, so 25 × 18 = 450
Answer: **450**

Splitting numbers

Make calculations easier by splitting numbers up as in the example below.

46 × 7 　 40 × 7 = 280
　　　　　6 × 7 = 42
　　　　280 + 42 = 322

Test yourself!

1 Multiply these numbers by 10:
   a) 34
   b) 809
   c) 2853

2 Multiply these numbers by 100:
   a) 24
   b) 362
   c) 4086

3 Double these numbers:
   a) 17
   b) 26
   c) 39

4 Use doubling to solve these:
   a) 24 × 4
   b) 36 × 4
   c) 43 × 8

Remember

For multiplying by 4, double then double.
For multiplying by 8, double, double and double!
Learn all the doubles of numbers to 100 (and then you'll know the halves too).

Mental division

Dividing by 10

To **divide by 10**, move each digit **one place** to the **right**.

52900 ÷ 10

TTh	Th	H	T	U
5	2	9	0	0
	5	2	9	0

Answer: **5290**

Dividing by 100

To **divide by 100**, move each digit **two places** to the **right**.

52900 ÷ 100

TTh	Th	H	T	U
5	2	9	0	0
		5	2	9

Answer: **529**

Dividing decimal numbers by 10

Decimal numbers work in the same way.
To **divide by 10**, move each digit **one place** to the **right**.

68.3 ÷ 10

H	T	U	.	t	h	th
6	8	.	3			
	6	.	8	3		

Answer: **6.83**

Dividing decimal numbers by 100

To **divide by 100**, move each digit **two places** to the **right**.

68.3 ÷ 100

H	T	U	.	t	h	th
	6	8	.	3		
	0	.	6	8	3	

Answer: **0.683**

Halving

Halving can help you to divide numbers.
To divide a number:

- by 2 – just halve it   e.g. **46 ÷ 2**   half 46 = **23**
- by 4 – halve and halve again   e.g. **96 ÷ 4**   half 96 = **48**,
                                              half 48 = **24**

- by 8 – halve, halve and halve again e.g. **128 ÷ 8**   half 128 = **64**,
                                              half 64 = **32**,
                                              half 32 = **16**

Once you have learnt some doubles, you automatically know some halves:

- double 59 = 118   half 118 = 59

Remember

To divide by 10, move each digit **one** place to the **right**.
To divide by 100, move each digit **two** places to the **right**.

Test yourself!

1 Divide these numbers by 10:
   a) 160
   b) 470
   c) 3840
   d) 7030
   e) 645

2 Divide these numbers by 100:
   a) 600
   b) 7800
   c) 9700
   d) 35 200
   e) 407

3 Halve these numbers:
   a) 68
   b) 78
   c) 96

4 Use halving to solve these:
   a) 84 ÷ 2
   b) 88 ÷ 4
   c) 96 ÷ 8

Written multiplication

When you multiply, approximate first. Here are some different methods of multiplication – you can choose any method you like.

392 × 8

	Th	H	T	U
		3	9	2
×				8
300 × 8	2	4	0	0
90 × 8		7	2	0
2 × 8			1	6
	3	1	3	6

> Multiply 300, 90 and 2 by 8 in turn. Then add. (You can multiply the numbers in any order!)

47 × 24

	Th	H	T	U
			4	7
×			2	4
		9	4	0
		1	8	8
	1	1	2	8

> Multiply 47 first by the tens digit, 2, which stands for 20. Then multiply by the units digit, 4. Then add.

153 × 74

	TTh	Th	H	T	U
			1	5	3
×				7	4
			6	1	2
	1	0	7	1	0
	1	1	3	2	2

> Multiply 153 first by the units digit, 4, and then by the tens digit 7, which stands for 70. Then add.

You might prefer to use the grid method of multiplication, like this: **354 × 12**

	300	50	4	
10	3000	500	40	3540
2	600	100	8	+708
				4248

Multiplying decimals

> **Calculate 2.34 × 2.6**

Approximation: 2 × 3 = 6
(then you needn't worry about the decimal points).
Now multiply as if they were whole numbers:

```
            234
         ×   26
234 × 20  4680
234 × 6   1404
          6084
```

The answer must be **6.084** rather than 60.84 or 608.4 because our approximation was **6**.

Answer: 6.084

Remember

Use whichever method you prefer, as long as you get the right answer!
You can treat decimals in the same way as whole numbers, **but:**

- approximate first
- **remember to put the** decimal point **in the answer!**

> **Multiplication** is easier if you **know your tables**. Take **one fact** that you don't know each day (e.g. 7 × 9 = 63) and **learn it**.

Test yourself!

1 Approximate first and then multiply these numbers:
   a) 53 × 12
   b) 67 × 84
   c) 257 × 18
   d) 305 × 27
   e) 69 × 723

2 Approximate first and then multiply these decimals:
   a) 4.3 × 7
   b) 5.2 × 6.4
   c) 4.9 × 9.5
   d) 3.25 × 8
   e) 6.27 × 3.4

Written division

Here are some different ways of doing written division.

692 ÷ 4

Approximation: 600 ÷ 4 = 150

This way builds up the answer using easy number facts.

$$100 + 50 + 20 + 3 = \textbf{173}$$
$$4\overline{)692}$$

4 × 100 $\dfrac{-400}{292 \text{ left}}$ ⟶ There are 4 lots of 100 in 692, leaving 292

4 × 50 $\dfrac{-200}{92 \text{ left}}$ ⟶ There are 4 lots of 50 in 292, leaving 92

4 × 20 $\dfrac{-80}{12 \text{ left}}$ ⟶ There are 4 lots of 20 in 92, leaving 12

4 × 3 $\dfrac{-12}{0 \text{ left}}$ ⟶ There are 4 lots of 3 in 12, leaving 0

Answer: 173

> If you know your tables you also know lots of division facts. Just turn them around!
> 7 × 9 = 63, so 63 ÷ 9 = 7 and 63 ÷ 7 = 9

Here are some other ways:

$$173$$
$$4\overline{)692}$$

4 × 150 $\dfrac{-600}{92}$

4 × 23 $\dfrac{-92}{0}$

This is a shorter version of the method above, where we start with 4 × 150 rather than 4 × 100. We can use whatever facts we know.

$$1\ 7\ 3$$
$$4\overline{)6\ ^{2}9\ ^{1}2}$$

This is called short division.
4 into 6 goes once, write 1 above.
Carry 2 to make 29.
4 into 29 goes 7 times.
Write 7 above.
Carry 1 to make 12.
4 into 12 goes 3 times.
Write 3 above.

Dividing decimals

Calculate 19.5 ÷ 5

Approximate first (then you needn't worry about the decimal points) 19.5 is about 20.
20 ÷ 5 = 4.
Now divide as if they were whole numbers.

$$0\ 3\ 9$$
$$5\overline{)1\ ^{1}9\ ^{4}5}$$

The answer must be 3.9 rather than 39 or 0.39, because our approximation was 4.

Answer: 3.9

Test yourself!

1 Approximate first and then divide these numbers:
   a) 575 ÷ 5
   b) 954 ÷ 3
   c) 927 ÷ 9
   d) 444 ÷ 12
   e) 1560 ÷ 24

2 Approximate first and then divide these decimals:
   a) 12.5 ÷ 5
   b) 66.9 ÷ 3
   c) 82.2 ÷ 4
   d) 53.2 ÷ 7
   e) 14.72 ÷ 32

Remember

It doesn't matter which method you use, as long as you get the right answer! Treat decimals in the same way as whole numbers, **but:**

- approximate first
- **remember to put the** decimal point **in the answer!**

Using a calculator

Your calculator will have some or all of these keys:

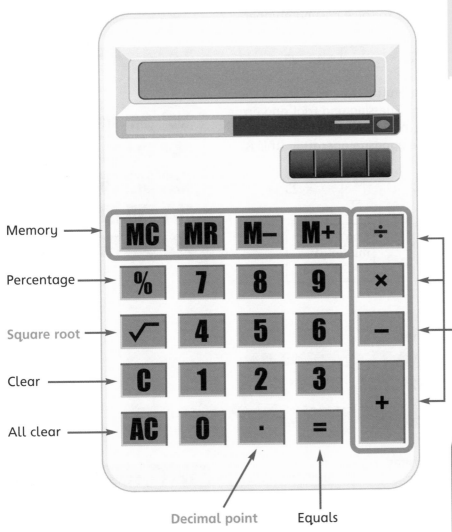

Memory
Percentage
Square root
Clear
All clear

Operations

Decimal point   Equals

Some calculators will be slightly different from the one shown. Check the instructions if you're not sure. See page 29 for more information on finding percentages with a calculator.

When using a calculator, always:

- do a **mental approximation** to estimate the answer
- **press the keys carefully** (put the calculator on the table and use your non-writing hand – then you can make notes as you go!)
- **check** that the answer matches your approximation.

Using the keys

The main keys you might use are:

- **Clear** – removes the last number entered. If you incorrectly enter 65 + 45 instead of 65 + <u>35</u>, press C and the 45 will be removed. Then press 35 = to get the correct answer.
- **All clear** – removes the whole calculation.
- **Percentage** – to find 45% of 20, press `2` `0` `×` `4` `5` `%` (The calculator 'divides by 100' when the % key is pressed.)
- **Square root** – to find the square root of 8649, press `8` `6` `4` `9` `√`

Test yourself!

1 Find the answers to:
   a) 35% of 70
   b) 65% of 50
   c) 32% of 60
   d) 85% of 90
   e) 73% of 150

2 Find the square roots of:
   a) 1225
   b) 1681
   c) 2704
   d) 4761
   e) 6084

Using a calculator

Solving missing numbers questions

You may be asked to use your calculator to solve missing number questions like these (see page 45).

$$39 \times \boxed{} = 195 \qquad 137 + \boxed{} = 182 \qquad \boxed{} \div 4 = 23$$

Think about each of these questions carefully. How would you solve them if you could **not** use a calculator? Guessing and trial and error aren't usually the best way of finding missing numbers. Instead, think about whether you could use the **opposite** operation (this is often called the **inverse** operation).

$$39 \times \boxed{} = 195 \qquad 137 + \boxed{} = 182 \qquad \boxed{} \div 4 = 23$$

| Don't guess – **divide!** $195 \div 39 = \mathbf{5}$ | Don't guess – **subtract!** $182 - 137 = \mathbf{45}$ | Don't guess – **multiply!** $4 \times 23 = \mathbf{92}$ |

Remember:

- **addition** and **subtraction** are opposites

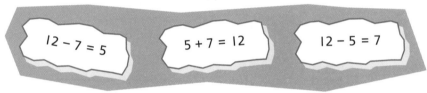

$$12 - 7 = 5 \qquad 5 + 7 = 12 \qquad 12 - 5 = 7$$

- **multiplication** and **division** are opposites

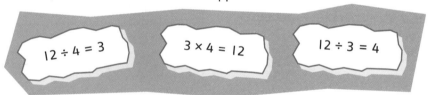

$$12 \div 4 = 3 \qquad 3 \times 4 = 12 \qquad 12 \div 3 = 4$$

These operations are opposites because they 'undo' each other.

Remember

Try using the opposite (inverse) operation to solve a missing number question:

- **addition** is the inverse of **subtraction**.
- **multiplication** is the inverse of **division**.

Test yourself!

1 Use your calculator to find these missing numbers:

a) $453 + \boxed{} = 986$

b) $365 - \boxed{} = 287$

c) $\boxed{} \times 45 = 855$

d) $1288 \div \boxed{} = 56$

e) $2016 \div \boxed{} = 63$

f) $\boxed{} \times 28 = 25.2$

g) $\boxed{} \div 6.5 = 89$

h) $27 \times \boxed{} = 86.4$

Solving problems

Word problems

36 people were on the bus. At the bus stop 17 got off but 12 more got on. How many people were on the bus now?

- Important numbers: 36, 17, 12
- Subtract 17 from 36 and then add 12
- Work it out: 36 − 17 = 19, 19 + 12 = 31
- Check against approximate answer.

Answer: 31

> Approximation:
> 40 − 20 + 10 = 30

Petrol costs 78.5p per litre. How much will 18 litres cost?

- Petrol is 78.5p for each litre.
- Multiply 78.5p by 18 to find the cost of 18 litres.
- Work it out: 78.5p × 18 = £14.13
- Check against approximate answer.

Answer: £14.13

> Approximation:
> 80p × 20 = 1600p or £16

Test yourself!

1 TVs are usually £392 each. In the sale there is a discount of £54 on each TV. What is the new price?

2 27 people were on the bus. When it stopped, 18 more got on and 23 got off. How many are on the bus now?

3 Tom buys a drink for 72p, a packet of crisps for 39p and some sweets for £1.12. How much does he spend?

Watch the units

In money problems, be careful with **pounds** and **pence**. Change the numbers so that they are both in pounds, or both in pence. Don't write £ **and** p in your answers, like £5.87p ✗

Watch out for other units in the same way (e.g., don't mix **metres** and **centimetres** or **litres** and **millilitres**).

Sunil buys a drink for 35p, a chocolate bar for 38p and a magazine for £1.45. How much change does he get from £5?

- He spends 35p + 38p + 145p = 218p
- He pays for this with a £5 note.
- £5 − £2.18 = £2.82
- Check against approximate answer.

Answer: £2.82

> Approximation:
> 40p + 40p + 150p = 230p,
> £5 − £2.30 = **£2.70**

When faced with a problem:
- Read it carefully
- Write down important numbers
- Decide how to work it out
- Get an approximate answer, work it out, then check.

Remember

Make sure all the numbers are in the same units when you calculate.

Solving problems

Remainders

When you are solving a problem that involves division, watch out for **remainders**.

How many 4s in 46?

Calculate **46 ÷ 4**, and the answer is **11 r 2**

Answer: 11 remainder 2

46 children are going on a trip. Each car carries four children. How many cars are needed?

Which is right?

| 11 r 2 | 11 | 12 |

Although there will be only two children in the 12th car, that car is still needed.

Answer: 12

46 photos are stuck in a photo album, with four on each page. How many pages are full?

Which is right?

| 11 r 2 | 11 | 12 |

Only 11 pages are full, because 11 × 4 = 44, with two spare photos.

Answer: 11

See page 16 for more information on dividing without remainders.

Test yourself!

1 I have saved £82 to spend on CDs. If a CD costs £9, how many can I buy?

2 A postman has 356 letters to deliver. He can fit 100 letters in his bag. How many trips will he have to make?

3 The football club has £60 to buy footballs. Each football costs £8. How many can it buy?

4 I have 160 photos to put in albums. One album holds 35 photos. How many albums can I fill? How many albums will I need?

Remember

Watch out for remainders and think carefully about what they mean.

Sometimes you may need to round up or down.

Exactly divisible numbers

Remainders happen because numbers are not always **exactly divisible** by other numbers ...

- All whole numbers are exactly divisible by 1.

- All even numbers are exactly divisible by 2. (All odd numbers will have a remainder of 1 when divided by 2.)

- All whole numbers that end in 0 are exactly divisible by 10.

- All whole numbers that end in 0 or 5 are exactly divisible by 5.

Solving problems

Missing numbers

The blue boxes below show calculations you could do to find each missing number.

$50 + \boxed{} = 101$

$101 - 50 = 51$

$12 - \boxed{} = 3$

$12 - 3 = 9$

$\boxed{} \times 5 = 20$

$20 \div 5 = 4$

$70 \div \boxed{} = 10$

$70 \div 10 = 7$

Now try these more difficult ones. You can use a calculator.

$315 + \boxed{} = 1001$ $\boxed{} - 87 = 38$ $67 \times \boxed{} = 536$ $703 \div \boxed{} = 19$

Finding the largest number

A good way to answer questions of this type, which use positive whole numbers, is to think about which will be the largest number:

- In every **addition** and **multiplication** question, the **answer** is always the largest number.
- In every **subtraction** and **division** question, the **first number** is always the largest number.

Once you have found the largest number, decide whether the missing number is larger or smaller than the other numbers:

- If it is **smaller**, use the other numbers to **make it smaller**, by **subtracting** or **dividing**.
- If it is **larger**, use the other numbers to **make it larger**, by **adding** or **multiplying**.

$\boxed{} - 87 = 38$

The first number is the largest. This is the missing number. You can use the other two numbers to make this largest number by adding 87 to 38.

Answer: 125

$703 \div \boxed{} = 19$

The first number is the largest, so the missing number is smaller. Now you use the other two numbers to make a smaller number by dividing 703 by 19.

Answer: 37

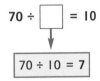

Test yourself!

1 Find the missing numbers:

a) $45 + \boxed{} = 86$

b) $25 - \boxed{} = 12$

c) $\boxed{} \times 7 = 42$

d) $65 \div \boxed{} = 5$

e) $50 \div \boxed{} = 2.5$

f) $\boxed{} \times 36 = 216$

g) $\boxed{} \div 12 = 6$

h) $48 \times \boxed{} = 36$

Remember

With **positive whole numbers** ... + and × make numbers bigger, − and ÷ make numbers smaller.

Formulae

A **formula** is a way of writing a mathematical rule that helps you to find answers quickly. Here are some formulae you may already know:

- **area of a rectangle = length × width**
- **volume of a cuboid = length × width × height**

Look at these questions:

> How many days are there in three weeks?

> How many days are there in six weeks?

> How many days are there in 50 weeks?

We can use a formula to help us answer questions like these:

number of days = 7 × *n* or number of days = 7*n*

The letter *n* stands for the number of weeks.

To answer the questions, we simply swap *n* for the number of weeks.

How many days are there in three weeks?

Number of days = **7 × *n***
$$7 × 3 = 21$$
Answer: 21 days

How many days are there in six weeks?

Number of days = **7 × *n***
$$7 × 6 = 42$$
Answer: 42 days

Using a formula

At a fair the entrance fee is £3 and each ride costs £2.

The formula for the cost in pounds (*c*) of entering the fair and going on *n* rides is

$$c = 3 + 2n$$

cost in pounds　　entrance fee　　2 × the number of rides

How much would it cost to enter the fair and go on five rides?

$n = 5$
$c = 3 + (2 × 5)$
$c = 3 + 10$
$c = 13$
Answer: £13

Formulae

The CD sale

It costs £2 to enter a CD sale and £5 for each CD.

CD SALE
Entry £2
CDs only £5 each

Write a formula to show the cost (C) in pounds of entering the sale and buying *n* CDs.

Answer: C = 2 + 5*n*

Dan enters the sale and buys four CDs. How much does he spend?

n = 4
C = 2 + (5 × 4)
C = 2 + 20
C = 22
Answer: **Dan spends £22**

Lucy visits the sale and buys nine CDs. How much does she spend?

C = 2 + (5 × 9)
C = 2 + 45
C = 47
Answer: **Lucy spends £47**

Curtley enters the sale and buys some CDs. He spends £37 in total. How many CDs does he buy?

C = 37
We need to find the value of *n* (the number of CDs)
37 = 2 + 5*n* so 5*n* must equal 35
5 × *n* = 35 so *n* = 7
Answer: **He buys 7 CDs.**

More formulae

Mrs Mason bakes *n* cakes. She gives four of them away. How many cakes does she keep?

Answer: **She keeps *n* – 4**

Tom has *y* rides on the Big Wheel. Dev has twice as many. How many does Dev have?

Answer: **Dev has 2 × *y*, or 2*y* rides**

Emily has 25p. She is given *y* pence. How much does she have now?

Answer: **Emily now has 25 + *y* pence**

Test yourself!

1 Look at the advert for the CD sale. Use the formula to answer these:
   a) Jennie enters the sale and buys 12 CDs. How much does she spend?
   b) Jessie enters the sale and buys 25 CDs. How much does she spend?
   c) Rob enters the sale and buys some CDs. He spends £52 in total. How many CDs does he buy?

2 a) Alice is given £*x*. She spends £7. How much does she have left?
   b) A book which cost £15 is reduced by £*y*. What is its new price?

Remember

We can use any letters, like *n, x, y, p, c* etc. to stand for numbers.

When a letter and a number are multiplied together, write them **without** the × sign then you won't get confused with the letter *x*:
e.g. 2 × *y* = 2*y*.

Measurement

When you are measuring, it is important to know what **units** and what **instruments** to use.

Metric units

You will need to know these ...

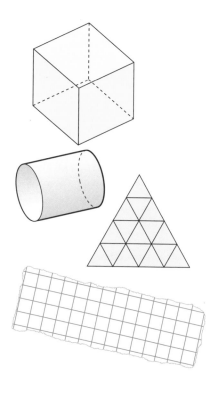

Type of measurement	Units (metric)	Instruments
Length including height, width, depth, perimeter, distance	**mm, cm, m, km** (millimetres, centimetres, metres, kilometres)	ruler, tape measure, trundle wheel, metre stick ...
Time	seconds, minutes, hours, days, weeks, years, decades ... etc.	watch, clock, timer, stopwatch ...
Capacity	**ml, cl, l** (millilitres, centilitres, litres)	measuring jugs, cylinders
Mass (Weight)	**g, kg** (grams, kilograms)	balance, kitchen and bathroom scales
Area	**cm², m²** (centimetre squares, metre squares)	squares, grids
Volume	**cm³, m³** (centimetre cubes, metre cubes)	cubes
Angle	° (degrees)	protractor/angle measurer
Temperature	**°C** (degrees Celsius)	thermometer

Test yourself!

I   Cover up the table on the left. What units would you use to measure:
a) time?
b) length?
c) mass (weight)?
d) capacity?
e) area?
f) volume?
g) temperature?
h) angle?

Units are things like kilometres or grams.
Litres or millilitres are the units used to measure **capacity**.
Kilograms and grams are the units used to measure **mass**, which is the mathematical word for weight.

Remember

Always write what units you are using.

Use the word **mass** instead of **weight** when measuring in grams and kilograms.

Measurement

Imperial units

Other measuring units, called Imperial units, are also used sometimes. Imperial units were once the only units used. Metric units were introduced because they are easier to use.

Here are some Imperial units you should know ...

Measurements	Units (Imperial)
Length including height, width, depth, perimeter, distance	inches, feet, yards, miles
Capacity	pints, gallons
Mass (Weight)	ounces, pounds, stones

It is useful to know how many of one unit makes up another unit, e.g.

Length
12 inches = 1 foot
3 feet = 1 yard
1760 yards = 1 mile

Mass (Weight)
16 ounces (oz) = 1 pound
14 pounds (lb) = 1 stone

Capacity
8 pints = 1 gallon

1 Cover up the rest of this page.
   Complete these sentences:
   a) Imperial units for length include ...
   b) Imperial units for capacity include ...
   c) Imperial units for mass include ...

2 Complete these:
   a) 1 foot = ... inches
   b) 1 mile = ... yards
   c) 1 stone = ... pounds
   d) 1 gallon = ... pints
   e) 1 pound = ... ounces

3 a) 1 foot is about .... cm
   b) 1lb is about .... g
   c) 1 mile is about .... km
   d) 1 gallon is about l
   e) 1oz is about .... g

Remember

Learn the names of Imperial units, their abbreviations and roughly what they are worth in terms of metric units.

Converting between metric and Imperial units

It is also useful to know roughly how many of one metric unit makes up an Imperial unit, and vice versa:

Length	Mass	Capacity
2.5cm is about 1 inch 30cm is about 1 foot 90cm is about 1 yard 1.6km is about 1 mile	25g is about 1 ounce 400g is about 1 pound 1kg is about 2.2 pounds 6kg is about 1 stone	500ml ($\frac{1}{2}$ litre) is about 1 pint 4.5 litres is about 1 gallon

  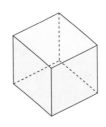 

Converting between units

It is important to know how many of one unit makes up another.

Make sure you know these:

Length
10mm = 1cm
100cm = 1m
1000m = 1km

Capacity
1000ml = 1l
100cl = 1l

Mass
1000g = 1kg
1000kg = 1 tonne

Time
60 seconds = 1 minute
60 minutes = 1 hour
24 hours = 1 day
7 days = 1 week
52 weeks = 1 year
365 or 366 days = 1 year
10 years = 1 decade
100 years = 1 century

> If you're having difficulty multiplying and dividing by 10, 100 and 1000, see pages 37 and 38.

Converting between metric units

Use these diagrams to help you convert:

× 1000
km — m
÷ 1000

× 100
m — cm
÷ 100

× 10
cm — mm
÷ 10

× 1000
l — ml
÷ 1000

× 1000
kg — g
÷ 1000

Test yourself!

Cover up the conversion tables.

1 Complete these:
   a) 100cm =
   b) 52 weeks =
   c) 1000ml =
   d) 1kg =
   e) 1km =

2 Convert:
   a) 35m to cm
   b) 750cm to m
   c) 6520ml to l
   d) 7l to ml
   e) 2500g to kg
   f) 3.25kg to g

Convert 56m to cm

Choose the correct diagram and insert the number.

× 100
56m — cm
÷ 100

56 × 100 = 5600
Answer: **5600cm**

Convert 8675g to kg

Choose the correct diagram and insert the number.

× 1000
kg — **8675g**
÷ 1000

8675 ÷ 1000 = 8.675
Answer: **8.675kg**

Remember

centi stands for **100th**, as in centimetre (100th of a metre).

milli stands for **1000th**, as in millimetre (1000th of a metre).

kilo stands for **1000**, as in kilometre (1000 metres).

Perimeter

Perimeter is the distance around the outside of a 2-D shape.

We measure perimeter in centimetres (cm), metres (m) or kilometres (km).

Imagine walking around this patio.

How far will you walk to get back to where you started? Trace your route, counting as you go.

The total distance would be 16m, so the perimeter is 16m.

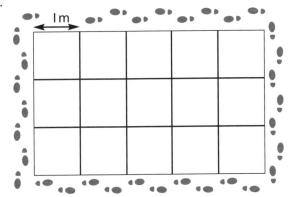

Find the perimeter of this rectangle

The perimeter is:

20cm + 8cm + 20cm + 8cm = 56cm

Answer: 56cm

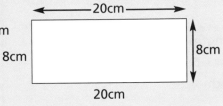

l stands for length, *w* stands for width.

The opposite sides of a rectangle are the same length.

This means we can find the perimeter when given only two sides, like this ...

The perimeter is:

15cm + 15cm + 10cm + 10cm = 50cm
or 2 × 15cm + 2 × 10cm = 50cm

We can write this as a formula in different ways:

2 × length + 2 × width or 2*l* + 2*w* or 2(*l* + *w*)

Find the perimeter of this shape

Using the formula 2(*l* + *w*)

2 × (12cm + 8cm)

2 × 20cm = 40cm

Answer: 40cm

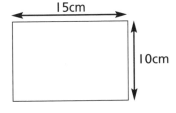

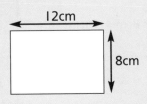

Test yourself!

1 Find the perimeter of these shapes:

a)   11cm

7cm

b)   13cm

9cm

c)   12cm

6cm

d)   15cm

20cm

Remember

We measure perimeter in centimetres (cm), metres (m) or kilometres (km).

The formula for finding the perimeter of a rectangle is:

2 × length + 2 × width or 2*l* + 2*w* or 2(*l* + *w*)

Perimeter

Perimeters of other shapes

Find the perimeter of these shapes

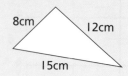

Add the lengths of the three sides.
Perimeter = 8cm + 12cm + 15cm
Answer: **35cm**

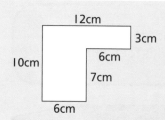

Add the lengths of the four sides.
Perimeter = 9m + 6m + 7m + 5m
Answer: **27m**

Add the lengths of the sides.
12cm + 3cm + 6cm + 7cm + 6cm + 10cm
Answer: **44cm**

Shapes with missing lengths

Sometimes you have to work out the lengths of some of the sides before you can find the perimeter.

Find the perimeter of this shape

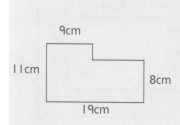

There are two sides with no lengths given.
Find them by subtracting:
19cm − 9cm =10cm and 11cm − 8cm = 3cm
Add the lengths of the sides:
11cm + 9cm + 3cm + 10cm + 8cm + 19cm
Answer: **60cm**

Word questions

The perimeter of a rectangle is 36cm. The shortest side is 6cm. What is the length of the longest side?

Draw a rectangle. Mark the two 6cm sides.
6cm + 6cm = 12cm.
36cm − 12cm = 24cm.
This is how much is left for the other two sides.
So they must be 12cm each.

Answer: **12cm**

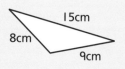

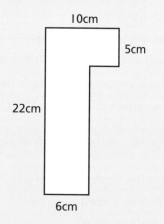

Test yourself!

1 Find the perimeter of this triangle:

2 Find the perimeter of this shape:

3 The perimeter of a rectangle is 48cm. The longest side is 19cm. What is the length of the shortest side?

Remember

To find the perimeters of shapes like these, **add** up the lengths of all the sides.

Area

Area is the amount of **surface** that a shape covers.

In a **2-D (flat) shape**, it is the **space inside the lines** or within a boundary.

In a **3-D (solid) shape**, it is the total amount of **surface of all the faces**: this is called surface area.

We measure area in **square units**, such as **square centimetres** (cm²) or **square metres** (m²).

Finding area by counting squares

We can find the area of a rectangle by counting the number of squares it covers.

Find the area of this rectangle

The area is 12 centimetre squares.

Answer: Area = 12cm²

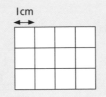

Finding area by multiplying

The rectangle above has 3 rows with 4 squares in each. 3 × 4 is 12. The area is 12cm².

Find the area of this rectangle without counting all the squares

Count the number of squares along the top (5) and the side (3).

5cm × 3cm = 15cm².

Answer: Area = 15cm²

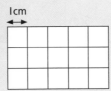

Find the area of this rectangle

Here the measurements are given for two of the sides.

Use this formula:

the area of a rectangle = length × width

or A = l × w

A = 8cm × 5cm = 40cm²

Answer: Area =40cm²

8cm

5cm

Remember

Area is the amount of surface that a shape covers.

We measure area in square units, e.g. square centimetres (cm²) or square metres (m²).

If length is l and width is w, the **area of a rectangle** = l × w

Area

Areas of right-angled triangles

Find the area of this right-angled triangle

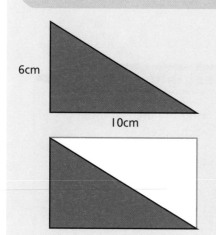

A right-angled triangle is half a rectangle.

So we can use what we know about finding the area of rectangles to help us.

Area of a rectangle = length × width
= 6 × 10 = 60, and we need half of this,
so 60 ÷ **2** = 30.

Answer: Area of triangle = 30cm²

Areas of other shapes

Sometimes you will be asked to find the area of shapes like these, made from two rectangles stuck together.

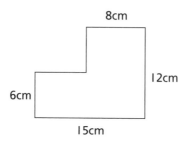

Split the shape into two rectangles. Find the area of each and then add the areas together.

6cm × 7cm = **42cm²**
8cm × 12cm = **96cm²**
           138cm²

Answer: the area of the shape is 138cm²

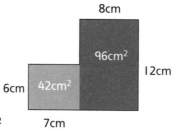

Find the area of this shape

Split into two rectangles
14cm × 6cm = **84cm²**
5cm × 4cm = **20cm²**
           104cm²

Answer: Area = 104cm²

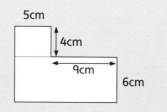

Test yourself!

Find the area of these shapes:

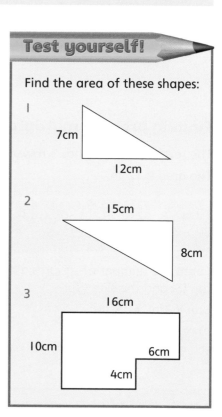

Remember

A right-angled triangle is half a rectangle, so the area of a triangle is half the length times the width.

The **area of a triangle** $= \frac{1}{2}l \times w$

Area

Area of 3-D shapes

The area of a 3-D shape is the total amount of surface on all the faces. It is often called surface area.

Find the surface area of this cuboid

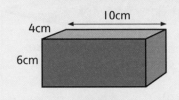

Imagine the cuboid opened out into a **net**.

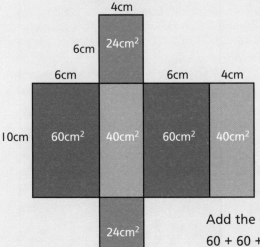

Find the area of each of the faces of the shape.

Add the areas together:

60 + 60 + 40 + 40 + 24 + 24 = 248cm²

Answer: The surface area of the cuboid is 248cm².

Find the surface area of this cube

All the faces are the same size.
The area of each is 6cm × 6cm = 36cm²

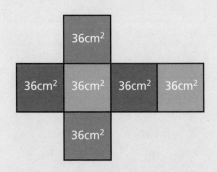

6 × 36cm² = 216cm²

Answer: **The surface area of the cube is 216cm².**

Remember

We can draw (or imagine) nets to help us find the surface area of 3-D shapes.

Find the areas of each face and add them together.

Volume

Volume is the space inside a 3-D shape.

We measure volume in centimetre cubes (cm³) and cubic metres (m³).

Finding volume by counting cubes

Find the volume of this cuboid

- count the cubes in **one layer**
- count **how many layers** there are
- multiply the number of cubes in one layer by the number of layers.

Answer: **8 × 2 = 16cm³**

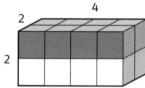

8 cubes

2 layers

1cm

Finding volume using length, width and height

Look at the shape again. Count the number of cubes along its height, length and width:

length = 4, width = 2, height = 2

Multiply the length by the width by the height to get the volume.

So 4 × 2 × 2 = 16

Volume = 16cm³

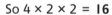

Find the volume of this cuboid without counting all the cubes

Multiply **l × w × h**

4 × 3 × 3 = 36

Answer: Volume = 36cm³

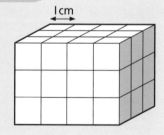

1cm

Find the volume of this cuboid

Multiply the length by the width by the height: 10 × 5 × 8 = 400

Answer: Volume = 400cm³

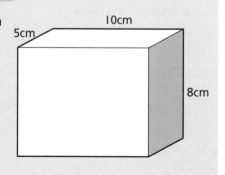

5cm

10cm

8cm

I Find the volume of these cuboids:

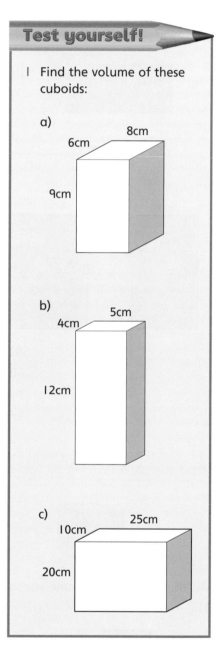

a)

8cm

6cm

9cm

b)

4cm

5cm

12cm

c)

10cm

25cm

20cm

Remember

The **volume of a cuboid =** length (*l*) × width (*w*) × height (*h*).

You can multiply the three numbers **in any order** – the answer will be the same!

Capacity

The **capacity** of something is the **amount it can hold**. We measure capacity in **millilitres** (ml) and **litres** (l) and in Imperial units (e.g. **pints** and **gallons**).

1cm cube

A millilitre of water fills one cubic centimetre and a litre is the amount in a standard pack of juice.

Learn this: 1000ml = 1 litre

Use the diagram to change between litres and millilitres (ml).

× 1000

litres   ml

÷ 1000

We can measure capacity in containers that have scales marked on them.

How much liquid is in each container?

- 1000ml
- 800
- 600
- 400
- 200
- 0

- 2 litres
- 1
- 0

- 500ml
- 250
- 0

Answers: 700ml   1500ml   400ml
(or 1½ litres, or 1.5 litres)

Look at page 58 for help in reading scales.

Look at page 58 for help in reading scales.

Test yourself!

1 What could you measure in:
   a) millilitres?
   b) pints?
   c) litres?
   d) gallons?

2 Estimate the capacity of:
   a) a bucket
   b) an egg
   c) a mug
   d) a teapot
   e) a bath

3 Change these amounts to millilitres:
   a) 7 litres
   b) 8.5 litres

4 Change these amounts to litres:
   a) 500ml
   b) 4575ml

Linking volume and capacity

Sometimes units of volume, like centimetre cubes (cm³) and cubic metres (m³), are used to describe capacity. This is because 1 litre of water is equivalent to 1000cm³ and 1ml of water is equivalent to 1cm³.

Remember

1ml of water is equivalent to 1cm³.

50ml and 50cm³ take up the same space.

Reading scales

The key to reading scales on measuring instruments is to look carefully at the numbers on the scale and to follow these steps:

Step 1: Choose **two adjacent numbers** (next to each other) and find the **difference** between them.

Step 2: **Count** how many **small intervals** (spaces) there are between these numbers.

Step 3: Work out, by dividing, **how much each** of these intervals is worth.

Fill in the number in the box

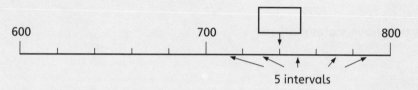

Step 1: 700 and 800. Difference = 100

Step 2: 5 intervals (spaces) between 700 and 800. Note it is the **intervals** we count, **not** the number of marks on the scale

Step 3: 100 ÷ 5 = 20.

Each interval is worth 20, so the arrow is pointing to **740** (700 + 20 + 20).

Practising reading scales

Practise reading the scales below. Write down your answers, then look in the pink box to see if they are correct.

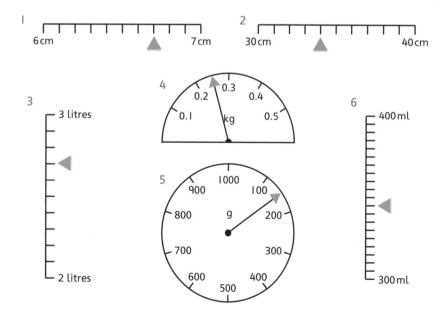

Test yourself!

1   Read these scales.
a)

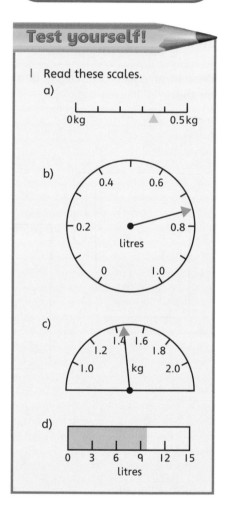

b)

c)

d)

Remember

To read a scale,
• find the difference between adjacent numbers
• count the intervals (**not** the number of marks) between them
• divide to find what each interval is worth.

Time

We measure time in seconds (s), minutes (min), hours (hr), days, weeks, months, years and centuries. Learn these units:

60 seconds = 1 minute	60 minutes = 1 hour
24 hours = 1 day	7 days = 1 week
52 weeks = 1 year	365 or 366 days = 1 year
12 months = 1 year	10 years = 1 decade
100 years = 1 century	1 millennium = 1000 years

Converting between units of time

Use the diagrams below to change between units of time.

× 24
day ⟶ hr
÷ 24

× 60
hr ⟶ min
÷ 60

× 60
min ⟶ s
÷ 60

Change 4 days into hours

Choose the correct diagram and insert the number.

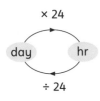

× 24
4 day ⟶ hr
÷ 24

4 × 24 = 96
Answer: 96 hours

Change 540 seconds into minutes

Choose the correct diagram and insert the number.

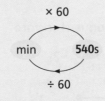

× 60
min ⟶ 540s
÷ 60

540 ÷ 60 = 9
Answer: 9 minutes

Days in the month

To remember the number of days in each month learn this rhyme:

'30 days have September, April, June and November,
All the rest have 31, save February alone,
Which has 28 clear and 29 in each leap year'.

Remember

For two equivalent times (e.g. 4 days = 96 hours), the **smaller unit** (e.g. hours) will have the **larger number**, e.g: 4 days = 96 hours

↖ hours are **smaller** than days
96 is **larger** than 4

Test yourself!

1 Cover up the table of units and complete these:
   a) 24 hours =
   b) 52 weeks =
   c) 10 years =
   d) 1000 years =
   e) 60 minutes =
   f) 100 years =

2 Convert:
   a) 5 days to hours
   b) 420 minutes to hours
   c) 8 minutes to seconds
   d) 144 hours to days
   e) 7 hours to minutes

Time

12-hour clocks

If you are using a 12-hour clock, you must **always** write a.m. or p.m., e.g. **11.20 p.m.** (evening) or **11.20 a.m.** (morning). This is because the hands of a 12-hour clock go round twice in one day, and you need to show which part of the day you mean:

- **a.m.** is for times between **midnight** and **midday (morning)**
- **p.m.** is for times between **midday** and **midnight (afternoon and evening)**.

a.m. or p.m?

24-hour clocks

A 24-hour clock uses the numbers from 0 to 24 to stand for all the hours in the day. 0 is midnight, and after midday the hours become 13, 14, 15, 16 etc. For example, 5 p.m. is shown as 17:00 and 9.30 p.m. as 21:30.

If you are using the 24-hour clock, you must **always** write the time using four digits, e.g. 16:45 or 09:10.

Telling the time with 12- and 24-hour clocks

Many clocks today are **digital** – they show the time using digits.

Some clocks and watches are **analogue** – they show the time on a circular face using hands.

12-hour clock	Analogue clockface	24-hour clock

'Quarter to seven in the morning'	'Quarter to seven'	'O six forty-five'

'Twenty past nine in the evening'	'Twenty past nine'	'Twenty-one twenty'

Test yourself!

1 Which of these are correct?
   a) six thirty in the morning is 6.30 p.m.
   b) eight fifteen in the evening is 8.15 p.m.
   c) ten past four in the afternoon is 4.10 p.m.
   d) quarter to ten in the morning is 9.45 p.m.

2 Convert these times to 24-hour times:
   a) 8.20 a.m.
   b) 12.15 p.m.
   c) 3.35 a.m.
   d) 1.05 p.m.

3 Convert these times to a.m. and p.m. times:
   a) 16:54
   b) 08:00
   c) 12:29
   d) 19:20

Remember

If you are using the 12-hour clock you must **always** write a.m. or p.m.

If you are using the 24-hour clock you must **always** write the time using four digits.

Time

Calculating with time

You may be asked to find how long a programme or event goes on for and when it started or finished. **Don't** use a calculator when dealing with time – you'll get the wrong answer!

If a TV programme starts at 9.20 a.m. and goes on for 1 hour 45 minutes, what time does it end?

Add or subtract the whole hours first and then count on or count back the extra minutes.

9:20 a.m. + 1 hour → 10:20 a.m. ...

then **count on** 45 min ... → 11.05 a.m.

Answer: 11.05 a.m.

If a tennis match lasts for 2 hours and 40 minutes and ends at 1:25 p.m., what time did it start?

1.25 p.m. – 2 hours → 11.25 a.m. ...

then **count back** 40 min ... → 10.45 a.m.

Answer: 10.45 a.m.

If the time now is 17:27, what time will it be in 3 hours 20 minutes?

17:27 + 3 hours → 20:27 ... then **count on** 20 min ... → 20:47

Answer: 20:47

Here are the start and finish times of some runners in a marathon

NAME	START TIME	FINISH TIME
Tom	10:20	14:35
Jill	10:25	14:05
Jack	10:30	13:20

How much longer did Jill take than Jack?

Find how long Jill and Jack took.

Jack took 2hrs 50min and Jill took 3hrs 40min.

Count on in minutes from 2hrs 50min to 3hrs 40min.

Answer: Jill took 50 minutes longer.

Test yourself!

1 If a TV programme starts at 1.20 p.m. and goes on for 3 hours 10 minutes, at what time does it end?

2 If I walk for 4 hours and 20 minutes, stopping at 13:35, at what time did I start?

3 If the time now is 7.15 a.m., what time will it be in 2 hours 40 minutes?

4 If the time now is 03:20, what time was it 5 hours 10 minutes ago?

Remember

Add or subtract the whole hours first and then count on or count back the extra minutes.

Timetables

Timetables are lists giving information about when things happen, such as train or bus times, TV programmes, cinema times etc.

The 24-hour clock is often used in timetables to avoid confusion over a.m. and p.m. To read a timetable, look along a row and down a column to where these meet.

Cinema Start Times for	Thursday		
	ABC	Multiplex	Odeon
Happy Days	14.20	15.45	17.50
The Game	19.50	20.40	21.40
Black Knight	18.30	19.45	19.30
The Shore	20.20	21.20	21.15

When does 'Black Knight' start at the Odeon?

Read across from Black Knight and down from the Odeon.
Answer: Black Knight starts at 19.30.

Look at the timetable below. Which train would you catch from Hawsker to arrive at Ashby at 11:00?

	train 1	train 2	train 3	train 4
Hawsker	08:30	09:45	12:00	14:30
Scarby	08:45	10:00	12:15	14:45
Egton	09:30	10:30	12:45	15:15
Ashby	10:00	11:00	13:30	16:00

Look across from Ashby to 11:00. What time is that train at Hawsker?
Answer: 09:45

Which train would you catch from Scarby to arrive at Egton at 12:45?

Look across from Egton to 12:45. What time is that train at Scarby?
Answer: 12:15

Which train would you catch from Hawsker to be in Egton at 15:00?

Answer: You would catch the 12:00 because the 14:30 would arrive too late.

Remember

To read a timetable, look along a row and down a column to where these meet.

2-D shapes

2-D shapes are flat shapes. They are called 2-D because they have 2 Dimensions, length (or height) and width. They have no depth.

2-D shapes are also called two-dimensional or plane shapes.

Shapes you need to know, and their properties

Circle – one curved side, with all points on the circumference the same distance from the centre.

Semicircle – half a circle, with one curved side and one straight side.

Triangle – three straight sides.

There are different types of **triangles:**

- **equilateral** – all the sides are of equal length and all the angles are equal

- **isosceles** – two sides are of equal length and two of the angles are equal

- **scalene** – none of the sides are of equal length and none of the angles are equal.

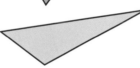

Pentagon – five straight sides

Hexagon – six straight sides

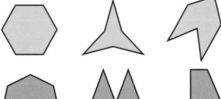

Heptagon – seven straight sides

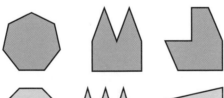

Octagon – eight straight sides

Other names you might come across:

Nonagon: nine straight sides

Decagon: 10 straight sides

Dodecagon: 12 straight sides

Parallel lines are the same distance apart along their length.

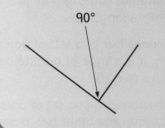

Perpendicular lines are at right-angles to each other.

90°

Test yourself!

1 Cover up the definitions. Can you identify these shapes?
  a) I have three sides of equal length and three equal angles.
  b) None of my three sides are of equal length and none my angles are equal.
  c) I have five straight sides.
  d) I have eight straight sides.

Remember

Triangle: three straight sides
Pentagon: five straight sides
Hexagon: six straight sides
Heptagon: seven straight sides
Octagon: eight straight sides
Nonagon: nine straight sides
Decagon: 10 straight sides
Dodecagon: 12 straight sides

2-D shapes

Quadrilaterals

All the shapes below are **quadrilaterals** – they all have four straight sides.

Quadrilaterals you need to know, and their properties

A **parallelogram** has two sets of parallel lines (see *a, d, e* and *f*, below).

A **rectangle** has four right angles. It is a type of parallelogram (see *a*).

A **square** has four right angles and four sides of equal length: it is a type of rectangle (see *d*).

A **rhombus** has two sets of parallel lines and four sides of equal length: it is a type of parallelogram (*e* and *d*). A **square** is a special rhombus (see *d*).

A **trapezium** has one set of parallel lines: one of the parallel lines is longer than the other (see *b* and *c*).

A **kite** has two short sides adjacent and of equal length, and two longer ones adjacent and of equal length (see *g* and *h*).

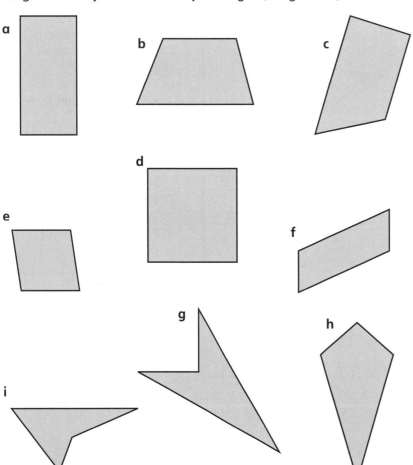

What about shape i? It doesn't match any of the descriptions above, so is just called a **quadrilateral**.

Remember

Any shape with four straight sides is a quadrilateral. Most can also be described using other, more specific names, e.g. parallelogram, rectangle, square.

2-D shapes

All 2-D shapes are either **regular** or **irregular**.

Regular shapes

A regular shape has all its sides the same length **and** all its angles the same size, like these:

Regular triangle
equilateral triangle

**Regular quadrilateral
(square)**

Regular pentagon

Regular hexagon

Irregular shapes

An irregular shape does not have all its sides the same length and/or all its angles the same size. These are irregular shapes:

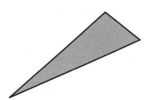

Irregular triangle
(not equal sides
or angles)

Irregular quadrilateral
(not equal sides)

Irregular pentagon
(not equal sides
or angles)

Irregular hexagon
(not equal angles)

Congruent shapes

Congruent shapes are identical in size and shape. They can be rotated but must be the same size and have the same angles. These pairs of shapes are congruent.

Similar shapes

Shapes are similar if they have been made larger or smaller but have not changed their shape, like these.

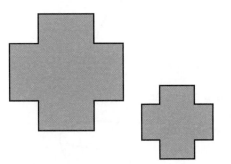

Remember

A regular shape has all its sides the same length **and** all its angles the same size.

An irregular shape does **not** have all its sides the same length and/or all its angles the same size.

3-D shapes

3-D shapes have **3 D**imensions, length (or height), width and depth. 3-D shapes are also called **three-dimensional** or '**solid**' shapes, even though they might be hollow.

3-D shapes you should know, and their properties

Shapes with flat faces

Cube   **Cuboid** (rectangular prism)

Prism (triangular prism, hexagonal prism, octagonal prism)
A prism has the same cross-section along its length. This cross-section can be any of the 2-D shapes. Think of a prism as a 2-D shape that has been stretched to make a 3-D shape.

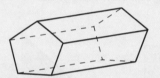

triangular prism   pentagonal prism

Pyramid (square-based pyramid, pentagonal-based pyramid)
A pyramid has a 2-D base, like a square, triangle or pentagon. The other faces are triangles and join together at a point or vertex.

A 3-D shape with only flat faces is called a **polyhedron.** The shapes above are all **polyhedra**.

Shapes with curved faces

The shapes below are **not polyhedra** as they have **curved faces**.

Cylinder (circular prism)   **Cone**

A coin is a 3-D shape and so is called a cylinder.

Sphere   **Hemisphere**

Polyhedra are described by the number of faces they have:
- a triangular-based pyramid has four faces and is called a **tetra**hedron
- a cube or cuboid has six faces and is called a **hexa**hedron
- an **octa**hedron has eight flat faces
- a **deca**hedron has 10 flat faces
- a **dodeca**hedron has 12 flat faces
- an **icosa**hedron has 20 flat faces.

Test yourself!

1 Cover up the text on the left, and name these shapes:

a)

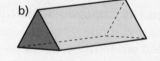

b)

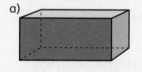

c)

Remember

3-D shapes have 3 Dimensions, length, width and height.

A **polyhedron** (plural **polyhedra**) has only flat faces.

3-D shapes

Properties of 3-D shapes

To describe 3-D shapes, you will need to know these words:

Face – a flat or curved surface

Edge – where two faces meet

Vertex – a corner or point

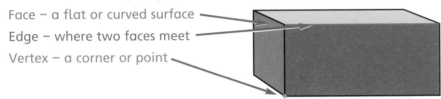

Name	number of faces (F)	number of vertices (V)	number of edges (E)	
cube	6	8	12	
cuboid	6	8	12	
triangular prism	5	6	9	polyhedra
tetrahedron	4	4	6	
square-based pyramid	5	5	8	
cylinder	3	0	2	
cone	2	1	1	
sphere	1	0	0	
hemisphere	2	0	1	

Relationship between faces, vertices and edges

For all **polyhedra** (flat-faced shapes) the number of faces plus the number of vertices equals the number of edges plus 2.

In other words,   **F + V = E + 2**

So, for example, for a cube,   6 + 8 = 12 + 2

This relationship was discovered by a mathematician named Euler and is known as Euler's Theorem.

Remember

A cube, it has six faces, eight vertices as well, it's also got 12 edges, and a cuboid has as well.

$$F + V = E + 2$$

Test yourself!

1 Complete these sentences:
   a) A face is ...
   b) A vertex is ...
   c) An edge is ...

2 Cover the table. Now try to picture these shapes in your mind.

   How many faces, vertices and edges are there on these shapes?
   a) cube
   b) cylinder
   c) triangular prism
   d) sphere
   e) tetrahedron
   f) cone
   g) hemisphere
   h) square-based pyramid
   i) cuboid

Reflection

Transformations are ways of changing or moving shapes.

You should know about three transformations: **reflection**, **rotation** and **translation**.

Reflection

To **reflect** a shape you need a mirror line, which might be horizontal, vertical or diagonal.

The reflection or new shape is called the **image**.

Watch what happens when the mirror line is **diagonal**.

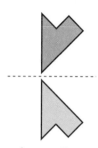 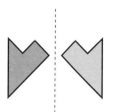

When reflecting a shape:

- Take one vertex (corner) at a time.
- Look where each is in relation to the mirror line. The image will be at the same point on the other side of the line.
- Twist the paper to make the mirror line vertical if this helps!

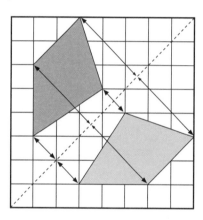

Reflection symmetry

A shape has **reflection symmetry** when it has one or more lines of symmetry. These shapes all have reflection symmetry.

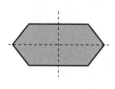   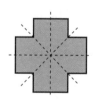

Remember

When reflecting a shape, take each vertex one at a time.

A shape has reflection symmetry if it has one or more lines of symmetry.

Schofield&Sims **Maths Key Stage 2** Revision Guide

Watch out with diagonal mirror lines. The first picture below is wrong!

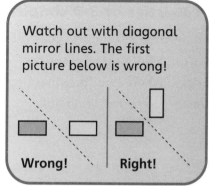

Wrong!   **Right!**

Test yourself!

1   Which pictures show a correct reflection of the red triangle in the dotted mirror line?

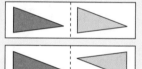

2   Give the coordinates of each vertex of the image of this shape when reflected in the mirror line:

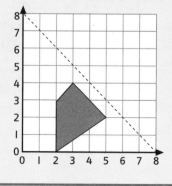

... rotation, translation

Rotation

To **rotate** (or turn) a shape you need a **centre of rotation**. This can be inside a shape, on one of its edges or outside it. You also need to know through what angle you are rotating the shape. The rotation or new shape is called the **image**.

These shapes have been rotated through 180°

  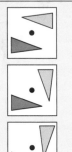

How to rotate through 90°

- Take one vertex (corner) at a time.
- Draw a line from the vertex to the point.
- Draw a new line at 90° to this line to find the new vertex.

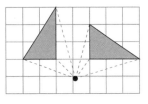

Rotation symmetry

A shape has **rotation symmetry** when it will fit into its outline in more than one way as it is turned through 360°. The number of times it fits is called the **order**. The shapes below all have rotation symmetry.

order 6   order 5   order 2   order 4   order 3

Translation

Translation means move or slide without turning.

A translation can be vertical, horizontal or diagonal.

These shapes have been translated

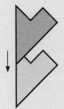 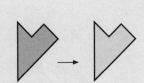 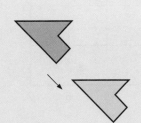

Test yourself!

1 Which pictures show a correct rotation of the red triangle of 180° about the point shown?

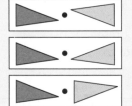

Remember

When rotating a shape, take each **vertex** one at a time.

A shape has **rotation symmetry** if it has an order of 2 or more.

Translation means moving or sliding without turning.

Diagonal translations are described by saying how many units across and how many units up or down the shape is moved.

two to the right, and one down

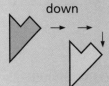

Coordinates

Coordinates allow us to **pinpoint exactly** where a **point** or **shape** is on a **graph** or **map**. Coordinates are written in brackets separated by a comma, like this (5, 12). They are an **'ordered pair'** of numbers which means the **order in which they are written** is important.

(5, 12)

(the **x coordinate**)
The **first** number shows how many places **across** to move on the **horizontal** axis.

(the **y coordinate**)
The **second** number shows how many places **up** or **down** to move on the **vertical** axis.

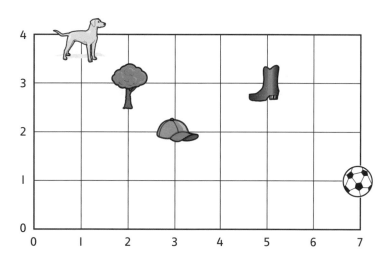

The tree is at **(2,3)**, which means **2 across** and **3 up**.

The ball is at **(7,1)**, which means **7 across** and **1 up**.

The boot is at **(5,3)**, which means **5 across** and **3 up**.

Drawing shapes with coordinates

You may be asked to plot several points, join them up and identify the shape you have drawn.

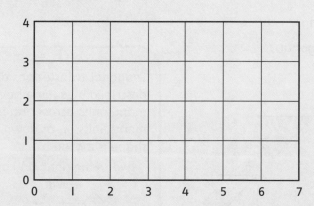

Plot these points: (0,1), (2,3), (4,1) and (6,3). What shape have you drawn?

Answer: A parallelogram

Test yourself!

1 On the grid to the left, what are the coordinates of:
   a) the dog?
   b) the hat?

2 Can you point to:
   a) (0,3)
   b) (3,0)
   c) (3,4)
   d) (4,3)

3 Look at these coordinate sequences. Give **three** more coordinates that will lie along the same line
   a) (1,4), (2,7), (3,10), (4,13) ...
   b) (3,5), (5,4), (7,3), (9,2) ...

Remember

When plotting or reading coordinates, we go **across** first, then **up** or **down**. ('Along the corridor then up [or down] the stairs')

Coordinates

Coordinates in all four quadrants

A grid has four quadrants. The 'first quadrant' in this grid has been coloured in. We can find the coordinates of points in all four quadrants by reading the axes, which run through the origin (centre point). Only those points in the first quadrant have coordinates that are all positive. The other quadrants use negative numbers (see pages 9 to 11).

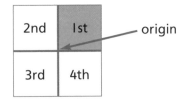

Example grid

The origin of the graph is at (0,0)

The position of:

A is (3,2)   B is (−2,2)   C is (−3,−2)   D is (2,−4)

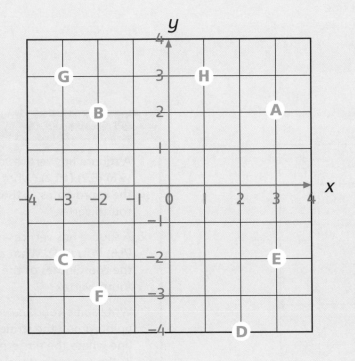

The x-axis is horizontal (across), the y-axis is vertical (up and down).

Test yourself!

1 On the grid, what are the coordinates of letter:
  a) E?
  b) F?
  c) G?
  d) H?

2 In which two quadrants are the x coordinates always negative?

3 In which two quadrants are the y coordinates always negative?

4 In which quadrant are the x and y coordinates always negative?

Remember

The x-axis is horizontal (across), the y-axis is vertical (up and down). x is a cross (across), y is high.

Coordinates

Working out coordinates using other coordinates

If you are given the coordinates of a shape and asked to find the coordinates of one of its vertices (corners), you don't always need to draw a grid. Look at this example …

> A square has vertices at these three coordinates: (4,3) (4,0) (7,0). What are the coordinates of the fourth vertex?

First sketch the square ──────────────▶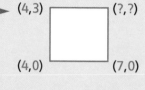

Notice that the **x coordinates** of points above or below one another are the same!

    4 and 4 are on the same vertical line
    7 and ? are on the same vertical line

Notice that the **y coordinates** of points along the same horizontal line are the same!

    0 and 0 are along the same horizontal line
    3 and ? are along the same horizontal line

Answer: **The missing coordinate is (7,3)**

Coordinates along straight lines

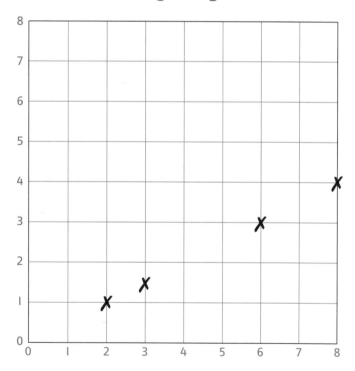

When any straight line is drawn on a grid, patterns in the coordinates can be found. In the grid above, the coordinates of points along a straight line follow this pattern: **The x coordinate is always twice the y coordinate.** All these points lie along the same straight line:

(2,1)   (3,1.5)   (6,3)   (8,4)

Test yourself!

1 A square has vertices at (6,6) (6,2) (10,2). What are the coordinates of the fourth vertex?

2 A square has vertices at (4,6) (4,1) (9,1). What are the coordinates of the fourth vertex?

3 Write some coordinates of points along the straight line where the pattern is: the x coordinate is always 3 more than the y coordinate.

Remember

The x coordinates of points above or below each other are the same.

The y coordinates of points in the same horizontal line are the same.

Angles

An angle is an amount of turn measured in degrees (°). Each angle is a fraction of a whole turn.

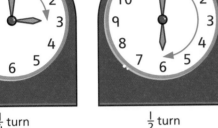

$\frac{1}{4}$ turn $\frac{1}{2}$ turn $\frac{3}{4}$ turn

Degrees, shown with the symbol °, are a more accurate way of showing an amount of turn.

There are 360 degrees in a full turn, written 360°.

360°

There are 360° in a full turn because, thousands of years ago, the Babylonians thought the Earth took 360 days to orbit the sun.

Instead of the arrow showing the turn, we use an **arc**.

Types of angle you need to know, and their properties

An angle less than 90° is called an acute angle.

An angle of 90° is called a **right** angle.

An angle between 90° and 180° is called an obtuse angle.

An angle of 180° is called a **straight** angle.

An angle between 180° and 360° is called a reflex angle.

Test yourself!

1 Cover up the text on this page. Can you remember the names of each of these?
   a) An angle of 90°
   b) An angle of 180°
   c) An angle between 180° and 360°
   d) An angle between 90° and 180°
   e) An angle less than 90°

2 What type of angle am I?
   a) I'm 67°
   b) I'm 328°
   c) I'm 180°
   d) I'm 100°
   e) I'm 90°

Remember

Acute: less than 90°

Right: 90°

Obtuse: between 90° and 180°

Straight: 180°

Reflex: between 180° and 360°

Angles

Angles in shapes

You might be asked to identify angles in shapes.

How many acute, right, obtuse and reflex angles can you find inside this shape?

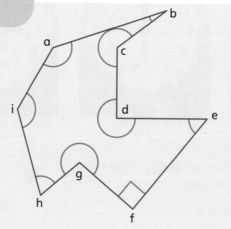

a) obtuse
b) acute
c) reflex
d) reflex
e) acute
f) right
g) reflex
h) acute
i) obtuse

Answer: acute 3, right 1, obtuse 2, reflex 3

Measuring angles

A **protractor** (sometimes called an **angle measurer**) is used to measure the size of an angle, like this:

How to use a protractor

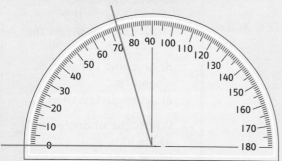

- Line up the centre with the point where the two lines meet.
- Turn the protractor until one of the lines is along a zero line.
- Count around from zero, in tens, until you reach the other line.
- Read the scale carefully.

Sometimes you might have to extend the lines with a pencil and ruler.

Remember

Don't be confused by the two sets of numbers around the edge of the protractor.

If the angle is acute, it will be smaller than 90°. If the angle is obtuse, it will be between 90° and 180°.

Test yourself!

1　How many acute, right, obtuse and reflex angles can you find inside this shape?

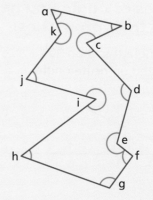

2　Measure these angles:

a)

b)

c)

Angles

Drawing angles

Draw an angle of 63°

1 Draw a straight line.

2 Place your protractor so that
   - the central cross is at one end of the line
   - the zero line lies on top of your line.

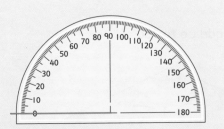

3 Count around from 0° and make a mark at 63°.

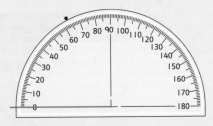

4 Remove your protractor and draw a line from the dot to the end of your line.

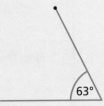

Estimating angles

You might be asked to estimate the size of angles without using a protractor, as below.

Estimate the size of these angles

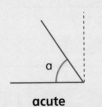

acute

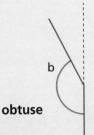

obtuse

First of all, decide on the type of each angle.

Angle a is acute, so it is between 0° and 90°.

Answer: angle a is about 60°

Angle b is obtuse – between 90° and 180°.

Answer: angle b is about 140°

Test yourself!

1 Draw angles of:
   a) 30°
   b) 45°
   c) 80°
   d) 125°
   e) 168°

2 Estimate, then measure, the size of these angles:
   a)

   b)

   c)

   d)

Remember

When measuring, drawing or estimating angles, decide what type of angle it is.

Angles

Calculating angles

There are many types of angle question where you are expected to calculate, rather than measure, the size of missing angles.

Angles in a triangle

The three inside angles of a triangle add up to 180°.

We can prove this by tearing a triangle into three pieces, with a corner in each.

Join the corners together to make a straight line. We know there are 180° in a straight angle, so there must be 180° in a triangle.

Find the missing angle

65° + 60° = 125°

180° − 125° = **55°**

Check: 65° + 60° + 55° = 180°

Answer: 55°

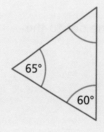

Angles at a point

Find the missing reflex angle

We know there are 360° in a full turn.

So, 360° − 42° = **318°**

Check: 318° + 42° = 360°

Answer: 318°

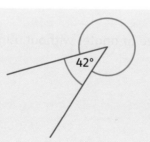

Angles on a straight line

Find the missing angle

We know there are 180° in a straight angle.

So, 180° − 78° = **102°**

Check: 78° + 102° = 180°

Answer: 102°

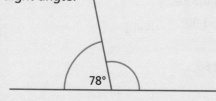

Test yourself!

1 Find the missing angle

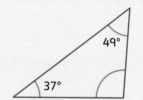

2 Find the missing angle

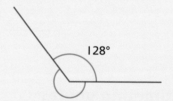

3 Find the missing angle

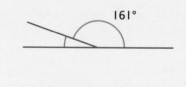

Remember

There are 360° in a full turn. There are 180° in a straight angle.

The angles in a triangle total 180°.

Probability

Probability is about the chances, or likelihood, of something happening, like whether we will win the lottery or toss 'heads' on a coin.

Probability words

When we are talking about probability we use words like:

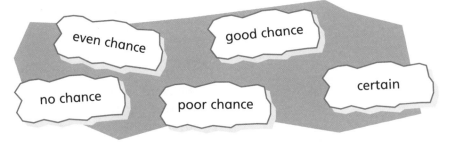

even chance   good chance   no chance   poor chance   certain

We might say 'I think there is a good chance of rain today' or 'I think City have a poor chance on Saturday'. We can write these words on a line where the likelihood increases as we move along it:

no chance	poor chance	even chance	good chance	certain

Now we can mark what we think on the line

no chance	poor chance	even chance	good chance	certain

I think there is a good chance of rain today. ⌐

We might use other words to show the same thing, such as:

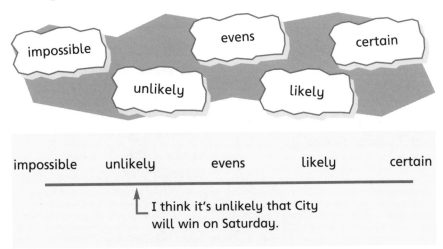

impossible   evens   certain   unlikely   likely

impossible	unlikely	evens	likely	certain

I think it's unlikely that City will win on Saturday.

Remember

Make sure you know these probability words: no chance, impossible, poor chance, unlikely, even chance, evens, good chance, likely, certain.

Probability

Equally likely outcomes

When you roll a dice the outcome will be one of six possibilities. The outcomes are 1, 2, 3, 4, 5 or 6.
Each of these numbers is equally likely so we say there are six **equally likely outcomes**. The probability of rolling each of the numbers is 1 out of 6, or $\frac{1}{6}$.

> **What is the probability of rolling a 4?**

There are six equally likely outcomes, **one** of which is rolling a 4, so the probability is $\frac{1}{6}$.

Answer: $\frac{1}{6}$

> The word 'event' is used to describe something that has happened or might happen.

> **What is the probability of rolling a number less than 3?**

There are six equally likely outcomes, **two** of which are numbers less than 3 (1 and 2), so the probability is $\frac{2}{6}$, which can be simplified to $\frac{1}{3}$.

Answer: $\frac{1}{3}$

> **What is the probability of rolling a 0?**

There are six equally likely outcomes, **none** of which are 0, so the probability is $\frac{0}{6}$, or 0. A probability of 0 means it is **impossible**.

Answer: 0

> **What is the probability of rolling a number that is more than 0 and less than 7?**

All the numbers on the dice are between 1 and 6, so the probability is $\frac{6}{6}$, or 1. A probability of 1 means it is **certain**.

Answer: $\frac{6}{6}$ or 1

> **What is the probability of rolling an odd number?**

There are six equally likely outcomes, **three** of which are odd (1, 3 and 5) so the probability is $\frac{3}{6}$, which can be simplified to $\frac{1}{2}$.

Answer: $\frac{1}{2}$

Test yourself!

1 How many equally likely outcomes are there if you pick, at random?
   a) a day of the week
   b) a month of the year
   c) a playing card from a full pack of 52 cards?

2 When you roll a 1–6 dice what is the probability of getting:
   a) a 3?
   b) an even number?
   c) a 7?
   d) a number greater than 2?
   e) a multiple of 3?
   f) a factor of 12?

Remember

When answering probability questions, find out the number of outcomes and whether they are equally likely to happen.

Probability

Using the probability formula

We can write probabilities using this formula

$$\text{Probability (P)} = \frac{\text{the number of things you want}}{\text{the number of equally likely outcomes}}$$

Think about the possible outcomes of picking, with your eyes closed, a red sock from a drawer containing 5 red and 2 blue socks. There are 7 equally likely outcomes because there are 7 socks. The probability (P) of picking a red sock is:

$\dfrac{5}{7}$ There are 5 red socks (the things we want)

There are 7 equally likely outcomes

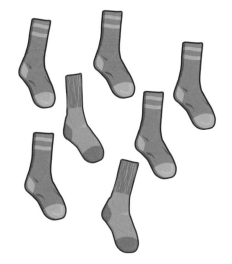

What are the probabilities of these events?

Choosing at random a day of the week starting with the letter T

Only 2 days start with T. There are 7 days so P = $\frac{2}{7}$.

Answer: $\frac{2}{7}$

Choosing at random a vowel from the alphabet

There are only 5 vowels out of 26 letters so P = $\frac{5}{26}$.

Answer: $\frac{5}{26}$

Choosing at random a red card from a pack of cards

There are 26 red cards out of 52 cards so P = $\frac{26}{52}$ = $\frac{1}{2}$.

Answer: $\frac{1}{2}$

Doing experiments

Another way of measuring probability is to do a mathematical experiment. To find the probability of rolling a total of 9 with two dice, we could throw two dice lots of times and record our results. The more times we throw the dice the more accurate our result will be.

Remember

Think carefully about whether an event has equally likely outcomes.

Test yourself!

I Which of these events have equally likely outcomes?
   a) a new baby being a boy
   b) rolling an even number on a dice
   c) picking a blue cube from a bag with 5 blue and 10 green cubes

Probability

The probability scale

Probabilities are often marked on a scale, which replaces words with numbers. 0 means the event is impossible and 1 means it is certain:

| impossible | unlikely | even chance | likely | certain |

0 _____ 1

What is the probability of rolling a 6?

It is unlikely, because there are six **equally likely outcomes** and rolling a 6 is only one of them, so the **probability** is $\frac{1}{6}$.

We can divide the line into the number of equally likely outcomes to show this …

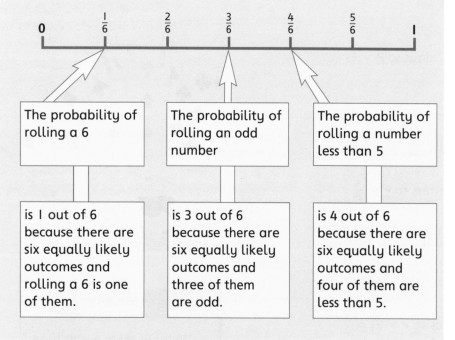

0    $\frac{1}{6}$ $\frac{2}{6}$ $\frac{3}{6}$ $\frac{4}{6}$ $\frac{5}{6}$ 1

The probability of rolling a 6

The probability of rolling an odd number

The probability of rolling a number less than 5

is 1 out of 6 because there are six equally likely outcomes and rolling a 6 is one of them.

is 3 out of 6 because there are six equally likely outcomes and three of them are odd.

is 4 out of 6 because there are six equally likely outcomes and four of them are less than 5.

I have eight cards, numbered 1 to 8. What is the probability of picking a 5?

Here we would split the line into 8.

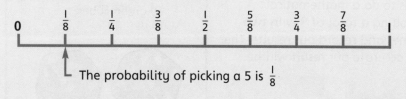

0    $\frac{1}{8}$ $\frac{1}{4}$ $\frac{3}{8}$ $\frac{1}{2}$ $\frac{5}{8}$ $\frac{3}{4}$ $\frac{7}{8}$ 1

The probability of picking a 5 is $\frac{1}{8}$

Answer: $\frac{1}{8}$

Test yourself!

1 Draw probability scales and mark the probability of these events. At random, what is the probability of:
a) picking a card with a diamond on it from a pack of cards?
b) rolling a 0 on a dice?
c) picking an ace from a pack of cards?
d) picking a red sock from a drawer with 3 red socks and 4 blue socks?
e) picking a red sock from a drawer with 5 red socks, 1 blue sock and 4 white socks?

Remember

A probability of 0 means an event is **impossible**.

A probability of 1 means the event is **certain** to happen.

Handling data

Frequency tables

A frequency table shows us how often something happens or how many things we have. To record data we can use **tallying**, where we group data in fives, like this ⌊⊦⊦⊓ = 5. We then write the frequency (or total) alongside. These tables are also known as tally charts.

A frequency table showing how many birds visited the bird table in one hour

Type	Tally	Frequency
Blackbird	⊦⊦⊓	5
Robin	II	2
Sparrow	⊦⊦⊓ II	7
Magpie	IIII	4
Greenfinch	⊦⊦⊓ IIII	9

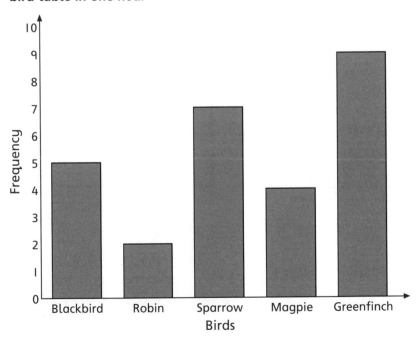

We can show this information on a bar graph (or block graph).

Bar graphs

Bar graphs, like other graphs, show information, or data, as a picture to make it more easily understood. Always label each axis and give your graph a title.

A bar graph showing how many of each type of bird visited the bird table in one hour

Remember

Always label each axis and give your graph a title.

Handling data

Using bar charts to show grouped data

Bar charts can also show grouped data. This is data that has been grouped together to make it easier to show.

The birthday months of a group of 11 year olds

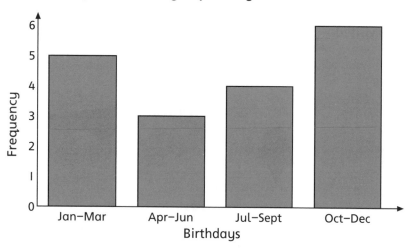

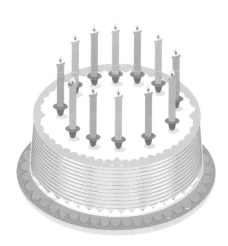

If this data wasn't **grouped** we would need 12 separate columns, one for each month. The data is called discrete data because it is about things we can count, like the number of people with a birthday between January and March. When we count the number of people with a birthday between January and March we are finding the frequency of that.

Bar line graphs

The birthday months of a group of 11 year olds
This bar line graph uses bar lines to show the same information.

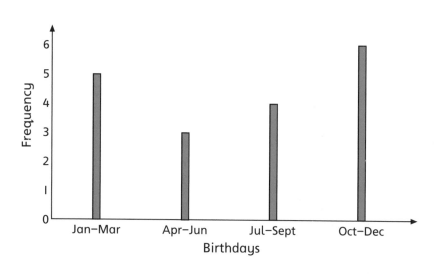

Handling data

Line graphs

Line graphs are another way of showing information, usually about what is happening over a period of time. Time is shown along the horizontal axis. Data is plotted and the points are joined together to make a line.

Here is some information about a hot air balloon flight during an evening:

Time	18.00	18.30	19.00	19.30	20.00	20.30	21.00	21.30
Balloon's height above ground in metres	0	250	300	400	450	300	150	0

A line graph to show a balloon's height above the ground

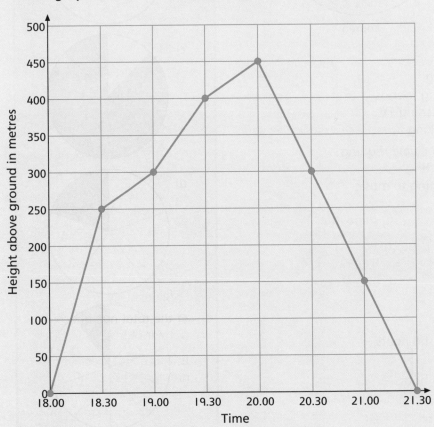

Test yourself!

1 At what time did the balloon first rise to:
   a) 250m?
   b) 400m?

2 On its descent, when did the balloon drop to:
   a) 300m?
   b) 150m?

3 At about what times do you think the balloon was at:
   a) 50m?
   b) 275m?

4 Could the balloon have gone any higher than 450m? Why?

For how long was the balloon above 300m?

Find on the graph when the balloon first rose above 300m (19.00) and then when it dropped below it (20.30).

Answer: It was above 300m for 1 hour and a half.

Remember

When answering questions about line graphs, be careful to read across and down from the points accurately.

Handling data

Pie charts

A pie chart shows information as different sized portions of a circle.

These pie charts show how two people spent their free time last Saturday. What fraction of their free time did each girl spend on each activity?

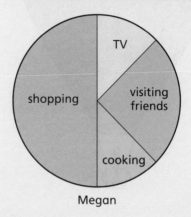

Megan

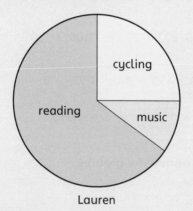

Lauren

Answer:

Megan spent: half her time shopping
about a quarter visiting friends
about one eighth watching TV
about one eighth cooking

Lauren spent: about two-thirds of her time reading
about one quarter cycling
about one tenth listening to music

If Megan had eight hours of free time last Saturday, how long did she spend on each activity?

Shopping – half of 8 hours –
Answer: 4 hours

Visiting friends – about one quarter of 8 hours –
Answer: 2 hours

Watching TV – about one eighth of 8 hours –
Answer: 1 hour

Cooking – about one eighth of 8 hours –
Answer: 1 hour

Pie charts are useful for showing proportions of a whole, like what fraction of your money you spend on different things.

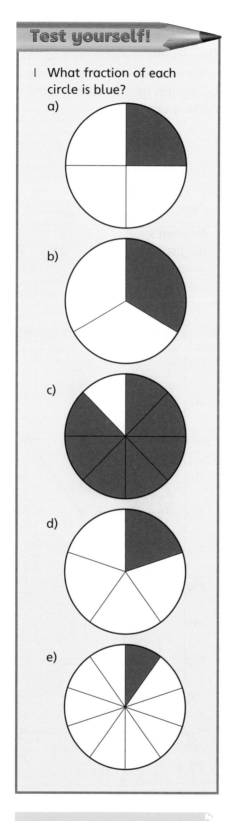

Test yourself!

1 What fraction of each circle is blue?

a)

b)

c)

d)

e)

Remember

Look carefully to see what fraction of the circle is shaded for each activity.

Handling data

Converting between currencies

There are two main ways of converting between currencies:

Using an exchange rate

For example:

> Exchange rate: £1 = €1.4

- To convert a number of pounds to another currency, **multiply** by the exchange rate.
- To convert another currency to pounds, **divide** by the exchange rate.

Convert £8.50 to Euros

Multiply the number of pounds by 1.4

£8.50 × 1.4

Answer: €11.9

Convert 17.50 Euros to Pounds

Divide the number of Euros by 1.4

€17.5 ÷ 1.4

Answer: £12.50

Using a conversion graph to get an estimate

A conversion graph has a straight line that shows the relationship between different numbers of pounds and Euros.

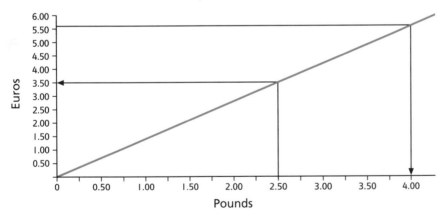

Convert £2.50 to Euros

Read up and across to convert from pounds.

Answer: €3.50

Convert 5.60 Euros to Pounds

Read across and down to convert from the other currency.

Answer: £4

Test yourself!

1   Answer these:
   a) Convert £17 to Euros
   b) Convert 22.40 Euros to Pounds
   c) Convert £8 to Euros
   d) Convert 10.50 Euros to Pounds

2   Use the conversion graph shown to estimate these:
   a) Convert £1.50 to Euros
   b) Convert 1.40 Euros to Pounds
   c) Convert £2 to Euros
   d) Convert 2.80 Euros to Pounds

Remember

To convert a number of pounds **to another currency, multiply** by the exchange rate.

To convert another currency **to pounds, divide** by the exchange rate.

Handling data

Range

The range of a group of numbers is the difference between the lowest and highest values.

> Here is a table showing Dan's recent test scores
>
> | 3 | 7 | 9 | 4 | 7 | 12 | 8 | 2 |
>
> The range is the highest minus the lowest score: 12 − 2 = 10

Sorting diagrams

Sorting diagrams helps you to organise and show information. The two main types are Venn diagrams and Carroll diagrams.

A **Venn diagram** uses circles inside a rectangle. The rectangle contains all the data. Each circle shows a part of the data.

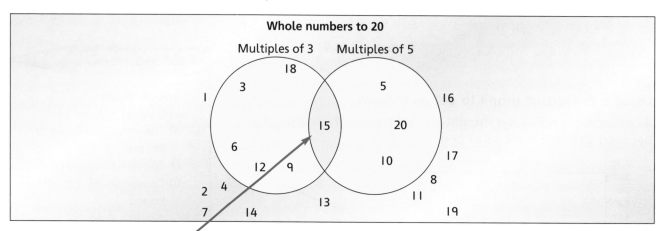

Whole numbers to 20

Multiples of 3   Multiples of 5

Where the two circles overlap is called the intersection.

The intersection contains data that belongs in **both** circles.

A **Carroll diagram** uses rectangles to show the same information.

	Multiples of 3	Not multiples of 3
Multiples of 5	15	5, 10, 20
Not multiples of 5	3, 6, 9, 12, 18	1, 2, 4, 7, 8, 11, 13, 14, 16, 17, 19

When drawing a Carroll diagram, put the word 'not' at the start of one row and one column.

Test yourself!

1 Find the range of these numbers:
   5
   17
   12
   21
   8
   16
   8

2 Sort the numbers up to 30 into both a Venn and a Carroll diagram using the labels 'odd numbers' and 'multiples of 5'

Remember

The range of a group of numbers is the difference between the lowest and highest values.

Mode, median and mean

Averages are values that give us an idea of a whole set of values. There are three types of average: mode, median and mean.

This list of numbers shows how many mobile phone calls Dean made on five different days.   10   2   7   9   2

to find the **mode** look for the **most** frequent, or common, value in the list …	to find the **median** put all the values in order and then find the **middle** value	to find the **mean** find the **total** of all the values and divide this by the **number** of values
10 ② 7 9 ②	2 2 ⑦ 9 10	10 + 2 + 7 + 9 + 2 = 30 30 ÷ 5 values = 6
• **the mode is 2**	• **the median is 7**	• **the mean is 6**

There can be **more than one mode**. The mode is also sometimes called the **modal value**.

If there is no middle value, the **median** is **halfway** between the two middle numbers. For example, for the set of values **3 5 9 10,** the median is **7** because it is **halfway between 5** and **9**.

This list shows the number of calls Mel made on 10 different days …

17   15   11   10   9   12   13   19   10   19

The **modes** are 10 and 19   (there are two each of these)

The **median** is 12.5 or 12½   (halfway between 12 and 13)

9   10   10   11   12   13   15   17   19   19

The **mean** is 13.5

17 + 15 + 11 + 10 + 9 + 12 + 13 + 19 + 10 + 19 = 135

135 ÷ 10 = 13.5

Notice that the averages don't have to be whole numbers!

Remember

An **average** is one value that gives us an idea of a whole set of values.

Mode – Most common value.

Median – Middle value (when put in order).

Mean – Means total divided by number of values.

Test yourself!

1 Find the mode
   10 8 5 9 5 7

2 Find the median
   9 4 3 7 5 1

3 Find the mean
   6 8 2 1 8 3 7

4 The mean of these cards is 6. What is the missing number?

   6   5   9   4   ▢

5 The mean of these cards is 7. What is the missing number?

   1   8   5   8   ▢

6 This table shows the amounts Kareem earned from jobs over six months. Find the mean, median and mode.

	A	B
1	Jan	£115
2	Feb	£125
3	Mar	£180
4	Apr	£153
5	May	£115
6	Jun	£119

Answers

Page 4

1
a) 300 + 10 + 2
b) 4000 + 800 + 30 + 9
c) 60000 + 9000 + 200 + 10 + 5
d) 2000000 + 100000 + 6000 + 300 + 80 + 7

2
a) 2 (two)
b) 20 (twenty)
c) 200 (two hundred)
d) 2000 (two thousand)
e) 20000 (twenty thousand)
f) 200000 (two hundred thousand)
g) 2000000 (two million)

Page 5

1
a) three hundred and fifty-one
b) four thousand, eight hundred and fifty-seven
c) two thousand and forty-one
d) eight thousand and two
e) fifty thousand and ninety-one
f) six hundred and fifty-nine thousand, two hundred and thirty-four
g) two million, four hundred and thirty-seven thousand, eight hundred and ninety-six
h) twenty million, two hundred and two thousand, and twenty

2
a) 5254
b) 61 591
c) 26 504 308
d) 1 100 101

Page 6

1
a) 2420
b) 3500
c) 5430
d) 3050
e) 6500

2
a) 2900
b) 8600
c) 9000
d) 9100
e) 63 000

3
a) 62 000
b) 35 000
c) 45 000
d) 75 000
e) 40 000

Page 7

1
a) 5690, 5700, 6000
b) 72 500, 72 500, 73 000
c) 30 900, 30 900, 31 000
d) 430 090, 430 100, 430 000
e) 2 652 990, 2 653 000, 2 653 000

2
a) 26.8
b) 18.6
c) 56.3
d) 60.8
e) 90.1

Page 8

1 92 716, 80 062, 67 293, 8502, 6291

2 48 602, 48 701, 50 001, 51 762, 54 351

3 62 071, 62 561, 62 809, 62 831, 62 835

4 3323

Page 9

1
a) 3
b) −2
c) −9
d) −5
e) −14

Page 10

1
a) −2, 0, 4, 6, 7
b) −9, −1, 2, 3, 4
c) −7, −4, −2, 4, 10
d) −15, −5, −2, −1, 7
e) −54, −23, −12, −6, −1

2
a) 8°C
b) 13°C

Page 11

1
a) 7
b) 12
c) 9
d) 5
e) 9

2
a) −7
b) −8
c) −8
d) −11
e) −12

3
a) −1
b) −1
c) 4
d) 7
e) 2

Page 12

1
a) 32, 39, 46 …
b) 43, 52, 61 …
c) 17, 11, 5 …
d) 4, −9, −22 …

2
a) 19, 25, 32 …
b) 27, 37, 49 …
c) 14, 7, −1 …

d) 62, 55, 49 …

3 Explanations of patterns such as:
1a) The sequence starts with the number 4 and each term in the sequence increases by a difference of 7 each time.
1b) The sequence starts with the number 7 and each term in the sequence increases by a difference of 9 each time.
1c) The sequence starts with the number 41 and each term in the sequence decreases by a difference of 6 each time.
1d) The sequence starts with the number 56 and each term in the sequence decreases by a difference of 13 each time.
2a) This increasing sequence starts with the number 5 and the differences between each term increase by 1 each time. The difference goes 2, 3, 4, 5 … and so on.
2b) This increasing sequence starts with the number 7 and the differences between each term increase by 2 each time. The difference goes 2, 4, 6, 8 … and so on.
2c) This decreasing sequence starts with the number 32 and the differences between each term increase by 1 each time. The difference goes 3, 4, 5, 6 … and so on.
2d) This decreasing sequence starts with the number 100 and the differences between each term decrease by 1 each time. The difference goes 11, 10, 9, 8 … and so on.

Page 13

1
a) (2), 7, 12, 17, (22)
b) (3), 11, 19, 27, (35)
c) (24), 18, 12, 6, (0)
d) (1), 6, 11, 16, (21)
e) (36), 29, 22, 15, (8)

2
a) (8), 6, 4, 2, 0, (−2)
b) (−3), 1, 5, 9, 13, (17)
c) (21), 11, 1, −9, (−19)
d) (−3), −7, −11, −15, −19, (−23)
e) (32), 20, 8, (−4)

Page 14

1
a) 32, 64, 128 … (×2)
b) 350 000, 3 500 000, 35 000 000 (×10)
c) 512, 2048, 8192 … (×4)
d) 1280, 5120, 20 480 … (×4)
e) 5184, 31 104, 186 624 … (×6)

2
a) 6, 3, 1.5 … (÷2)
b) 410, 41, 4.1 … (÷10)

c) 64, 12.8, 2.56 … (÷5)
d) 320, 160, 80 … (÷2)
e) 0.000246, 0.00000246, 0.0000000246 … (÷100)

3
a) 50, 500, 5000
b) 640, 6400, 64 000
c) 870, 8700, 87 000
d) 2380, 23 800, 238 000
e) 5340, 53 400, 534 000

4
a) 600, 60, 6
b) 720, 72, 7.2
c) 6900, 690, 69
d) 126.4, 12.64, 1.264
e) 650.3, 65.03, 6.503

Page 15

1
a) 68, 140
b) 18, 19
c) 55, 111
d) 22, 21
e) 0.75, 1.5

Page 16

1

12	12
24	36
32	21
36	28
45	56

2
1, 2, 3, 5, 6, 10, 15, 30

3
1, 5, 25

4
1, 2, 3, 4, 6, 8, 12, 16, 24, 32, 48, 96

5
92, 740, 332

6
96, 240, 216

Page 17

1
315, 594

2
84, 96, 606

3
117, 459, 702

4
67, 73, 91, 107, 473

Page 18

1
1, 4, 9, 16, 25, 36, 49, 64, 81, 100, 121, 144

2
a) 8
b) 11
c) 12

3
a) 39
b) 57
c) 41

4
5041